Your Bike

About the Book

This guidebook reveals the world of bikes from the inside out, presenting detailed, yet concise instructions for motorcycle maintenance. Author Chet Cunningham offers inside tips on how to select the right bike and how to customize one. Helpful to those who already own and ride motorcycles, YOUR BIKE will point the newcomer in the direction of safe and knowledgeable driving.

YOUR BIKE
HOW TO KEEP YOUR MOTORCYCLE RUNNING

CHET CUNNINGHAM

G. P. PUTNAM'S SONS, NEW YORK

All photographs in this book are by the author, except as follows: page 47 courtesy of Benelli; pages 70 and 100 courtesy of BMW; pages 2, 8, 40, 55, 62, 72, 112, 117, and 118 courtesy of Harley-Davidson; pages 52, 114, and 115 courtesy of Hodaka; pages 50 and 115 courtesy of Kawasaki; pages 74 and 75 courtesy of Paulson Manufacturing Corporation; pages 47, 49, 51, and 111 courtesy of Suzuki; and pages 57 and 61 courtesy of Yamaha.

Copyright © 1975 by Chet Cunningham
All rights reserved. Published simultaneously in
Canada by Longman Canada Limited, Toronto.
SBN: GB-399-60925-3
SBN: TR-399-20435-0
Library of Congress Catalog Card Number: 74-16626
PRINTED IN THE UNITED STATES OF AMERICA

Contents

Introduction   9
Section 1: Motorcycle Maintenance   11
Section 2: Minor Bike Repairs   25
Section 3: Trouble-Fixing Your Bike   39
Section 4: Accessories and Improvements   67
Section 5: Know Your Machine   79
Section 6: Which Motorcycle for You?   109
Index   121

Your Bike

Introduction

You feel the slap of your bike against your leg as you lean into a corner. You feel the surge of power and the sense of freedom as you get away on your own. You are on a motorcycle, and no matter where you are going or why, just riding it is pure fun.

Motorcycles are not just for the big guys. Today an estimated 200,000 riders between eight and fourteen own some kind of motor bike. But even if you aren't at the riding stage yet, you can still learn how to care for one and how to fix one. Then when you get your bike, you'll be a jump ahead.

Say your dad has a bike he rides after work and on weekends. If you can help him when he services it and cleans it, when he checks the plug and oil level and cleans the air filter, he'll notice, and you may well get your own bike sooner.

Don't worry if you're no natural mechanic. We all have to start someplace. A few simple tools will help you make many repairs. Doing them will give you the feel of the machine and prepare you for tougher projects.

If you're concerned about money, remember, the more small jobs you do, the less it will cost for the big service jobs at the dealership.

A list of minor repairs you can do on a motorcycle is included. These are a little more difficult and more advanced than the maintenance jobs. Most will involve some tools and some thought to do them properly. To help you, we'll give step-by-step suggestions.

One of the big problems with engines is what to do when something goes wrong. This is often called "trouble-fixing." One section shows ways to diagnose problems and standard ways of solving them.

Safety experts say that a motorcycle is inherently more dangerous than a four-wheel vehicle. On a motorcycle you must maintain your balance; you are limited in the sharpness of any turn and restricted in braking ability. You are a high injury risk since you have no steel shell protecting you. So before you get on a motorcycle, believe that it is by its very structure a more dangerous form of transportation than driving a car. When you understand this, you'll learn to ride your bike safely and avoid the built-in dangers.

Section 1

Motorcycle Maintenance

You probably know a lot about bicycles, how to tear them down and reassemble them, how to get the derailer on properly and where the various sprockets on a ten-speed fit. Working on a motorcycle is tougher than a bike, but much is similar. Both have wheels, rims, tires, chains, sprockets, frame, front fork, and handlebars. The key difference is the motor, which makes a motorcycle bigger, heavier, and more intricate.

You can work on a bike without being a mechanic. Most of us aren't very good with tools. Only a few are natural wrench jockeys—the rest lunge along, skinning knuckles, rounding off bolt heads, and trying to turn screws the wrong way. Try it. You'll be surprised how easy regular maintenance projects for bikes are. (We'll say "bikes" when we're referring to motorcycles. It's a shorter word, and those who ride these rigs call them bikes.)

Nearly fifty brand names of bikes are sold in this country, though the number varies from year to year. There are several models under most brand names, but they are a lot alike and the maintenance tasks are similar.

A lot of guys start riding a machine with an engine designation of 125. That simply means it has about 125 cubic centimeters of piston displacement. Since we can't show you all the models or makes, we've selected a Harley-Davidson TX-125 to serve as a model bike. It is a combination street machine and trail rig, having a high front fender, engine protection plate, and high-mounted exhaust usually associated with trail machines. However, it is also equipped with horn, front and back turn signals, two-passenger seat, and rear-rider foot rests that many street machines have.

Most of its features will be similar to those on your bike. The minor differences will not alter servicing and maintenance procedures. You can take the main idea and with your owner's manual come up with good service work on your bike.

Now, what are some of these maintenance jobs that you can do to help convince your dad that you're ready for a bike of your own? Here are eight suggestions, with details and pictures all directed at the Harley-Davidson TX-125.

1 Air cleaner

Every bike has an air cleaner. Its purpose is to filter the air passing into the combustion chamber and remove dust and dirt. Inside a piston dirt acts as grit, gets into the oil, and wears down close-fitting metal-to-metal working parts.

To service the air cleaner, first take off the air cleaner cover nut,

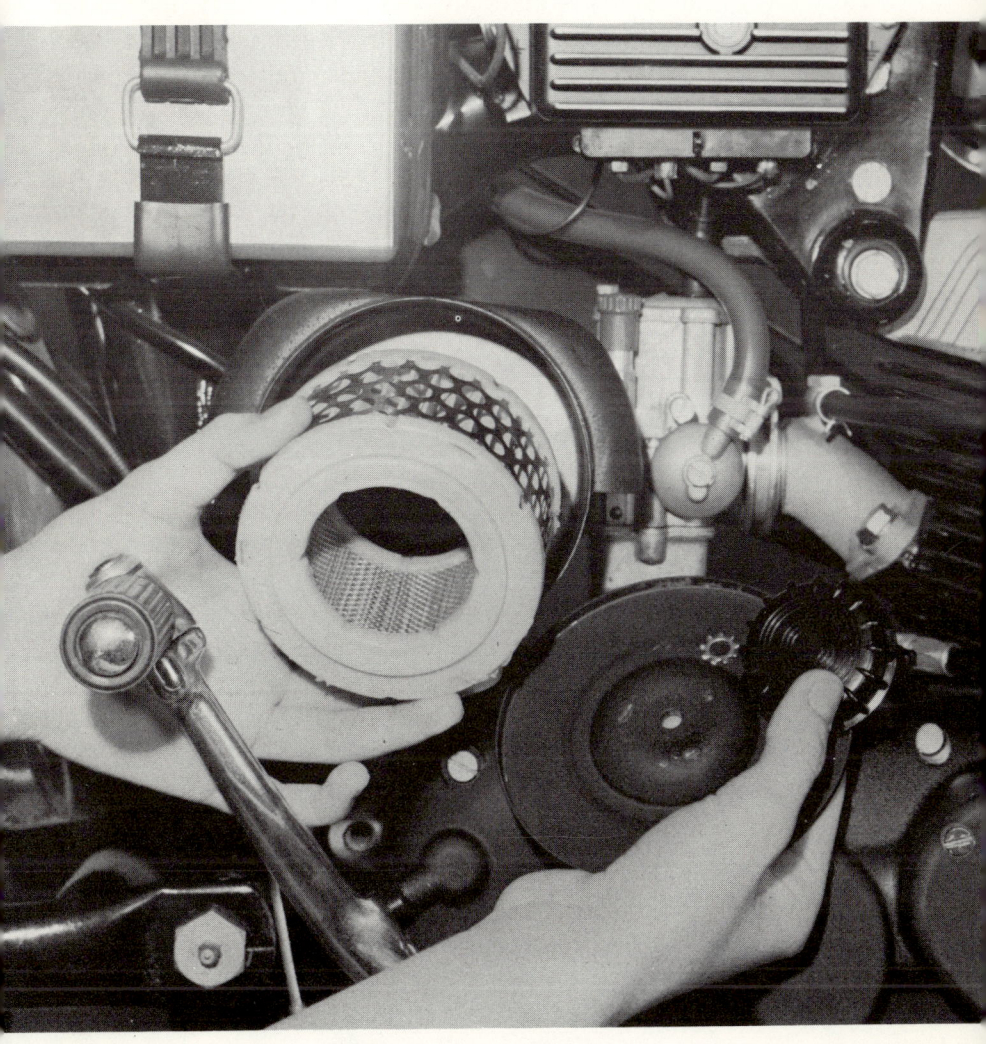

Removing the air cleaner.

then the cover. The round, pleated-paper, plastic-bound air filter comes out easily. If it looks dirty, tap it sharply on a hard surface.

If you blow it clean with an air hose, use a low-pressure nozzle and blow from inside the tube outward. This type of air cleaner should not be immersed in solvent, but some kinds can be washed in solvent or hot water and nonsudsing detergent. Check your owner's manual.

On most bikes you should inspect your air filter every 1,000 miles or more frequently after going through dusty conditions or doing a lot of off-road riding. A dirt-clogged air filter stops the air flow into the combustion chamber and your bike is oxygen-starved, running excessively rich in mixture. This can result in loss of engine power, overheating, and excessive fuel consumption.

2 Fuel strainer

One part that can stand frequent removal and cleaning is the fuel filter screen, situated at the end of the gasoline line connection on the carburetor bowl.

This screen should be removed and cleaned when you feel any hesitation that could mean a blocked fuel supply. See that the gas flows freely from the supply valve before closing the valve to remove the screen.

In some cases your bike may still show signs of irregular carburetion. This means there is some problem in your carburetor, but since it's a highly developed piece of equipment, it's best to leave it alone and take your bike back to your dealer, whose experienced men will remove, clean, and adjust all of the carburetor's many operations to get your bike running correctly again.

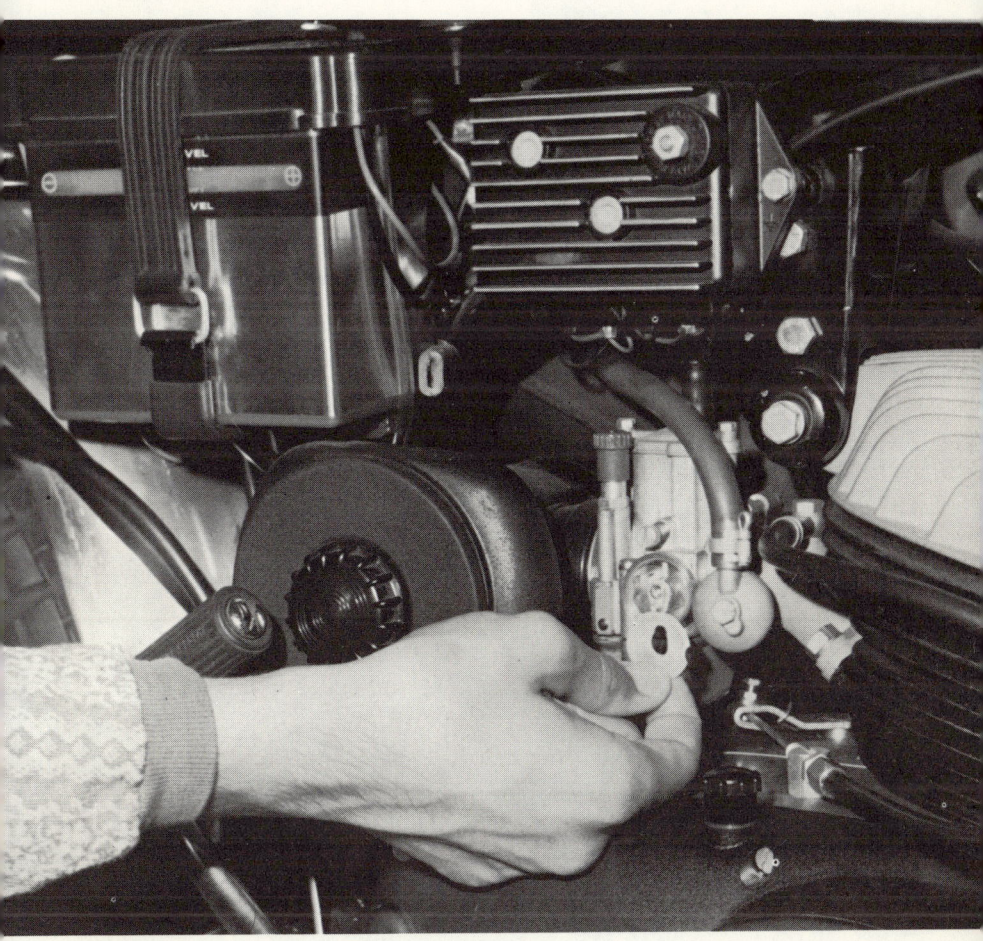

The gas strainer.

The oil pump.

3 Lubricating oil pump

Many older motorcycles in this 100 and 125cc class have the lubrication oil for the engine added to the gasoline. On the Harley-Davidson TX-125 and many new machines the lubrication is done with an oil pump. The oil pump, located inside the right crankcase cover, is driven by the engine crankshaft. It delivers small quantities of oil into the manifold to provide direct engine lubrication. The amount of oil delivered is controlled by the throttle grip. So the faster you throttle up the engine, the more oil is provided for the greater needs of the machine.

Your only maintenance work here is to see that the reference mark and the maximum flow mark are both in line when the throttle is fully opened. Your oil consumption at this setting will be from 4 percent to 5 percent of your gasoline use.

4 Check your spark plug

Every thousand miles you should remove the spark plug and inspect it. If it is in good condition you need only adjust the gap before putting it back.

First disconnect the snap-on wire connection by pulling up on the rubber cap. Then clean away any grease or dirt from around the plug base so nothing falls into the cylinder when the plug is removed. Use a special plug wrench or deep socket to take out the plug.

Look over the spark plug carefully to double-check the carburetor's oil/gas mix and the general condition of your engine.

If your plug shows a rust brown to tan powdery deposit, that means your engine's in good tune.

If a light brown, dry, glassy type of deposit can be seen on your plug, it indicates an overheating condition. This may have resulted from misfiring at high speeds, too lean an air-fuel mixture, a hot-running engine, or improper ignition timing.

During your inspection of the plug, check to see if it has any cracks in the insulator or if the electrode is eroded. If so, your plug should be replaced with one of identical type and make. It's best to buy plugs from your authorized and franchised dealer for your make of bike.

If the plug is in good condition, clean it with a sand blaster. Many filling stations have this machine, which uses sand propelled by air pressure to scour the firing end of your plug. Then take a wire gauge and check the spark-plug gap. This should be set at between .025 and .030 of an inch. If it's too wide for your wire, squeeze the outer electrode lower with pliers. But do it carefully.

Adjust the gap until a slight drag on the wire gauge is noted when it passes between the electrodes.

Look at the plug's threads and then the threads in the cylinder head. Apply a small amount of penetrating oil with your finger on the head threads to loosen any carbon deposits, then wipe clean.

Put the regapped or new plug in the hole after fitting it with a new plug gasket. Turn with your fingers until it is tight, then use a spark-plug wrench to tighten until the gasket is compressed. Avoid over-tightening any spark plug.

5   Inspect circuit-breaker points

You should inspect the gap and condition of the circuit-breaker points every 2,000 miles. Doing this is not hard but will require tools. First loosen the bolt holding on the gear-shift lever and pull it off the post, then remove the screws that hold on the left crankcase cover. This is directly behind the gear-shift lever at your left foot when sitting on the bike.

The points, lock screw, and adjustment slot will show in one of two windows on the rotor on the upper right side. The point contact surfaces should appear clean, dull gray, slightly rough. If the points are dirty but otherwise in good condition, clean them with a strip of hard-surfaced, heavy paper saturated with clean white gasoline. If the points are deeply pitted or badly burned, you should replace them with a new point assembly rather than try to file them smooth.

To have your points adjusted we suggest you see your franchised dealer.

Checking the circuit breaker points.

6 Removing the carbon

After 5,000 miles your engine may become sluggish and show loss of power. Is so, the carbon needs to be cleaned from the cylinder exhaust port and soot removed from the muffler and exhaust pipe.

The exhaust port is that place where your muffler attaches to the cylinder. Do this job by removing the exhaust pipe from the exhaust port. Move the piston to bottom dead center by rolling the bike while it is in gear. Then carefully scrape all the carbon from the exhaust port and wipe all the loose carbon particles from the exhaust port.

When you clean the muffler, take the core of the muffler from the shell. This can be done by removing a retainer screw and pulling the core with pliers. Check your owner's manual for your bike's procedure here.

Soak the parts in carbon solvent and clean with a wire brush. When you get the parts clean of all soot, reassemble the muffler. Be sure you reassemble it properly, and follow manual specifications carefully.

After extended periods of riding carbon buildup will take place in your combustion chamber causing the engine to knock and lose power. Removing this carbon is a job for the mechanic at your franchised dealership.

7 Battery servicing

Many smaller motorcycles have no batteries, but most of the newer ones do. It is not the miles of service that affect the life of your bike battery, rather it is the care it is given.

At least once a month or more often if the bike is ridden a lot or

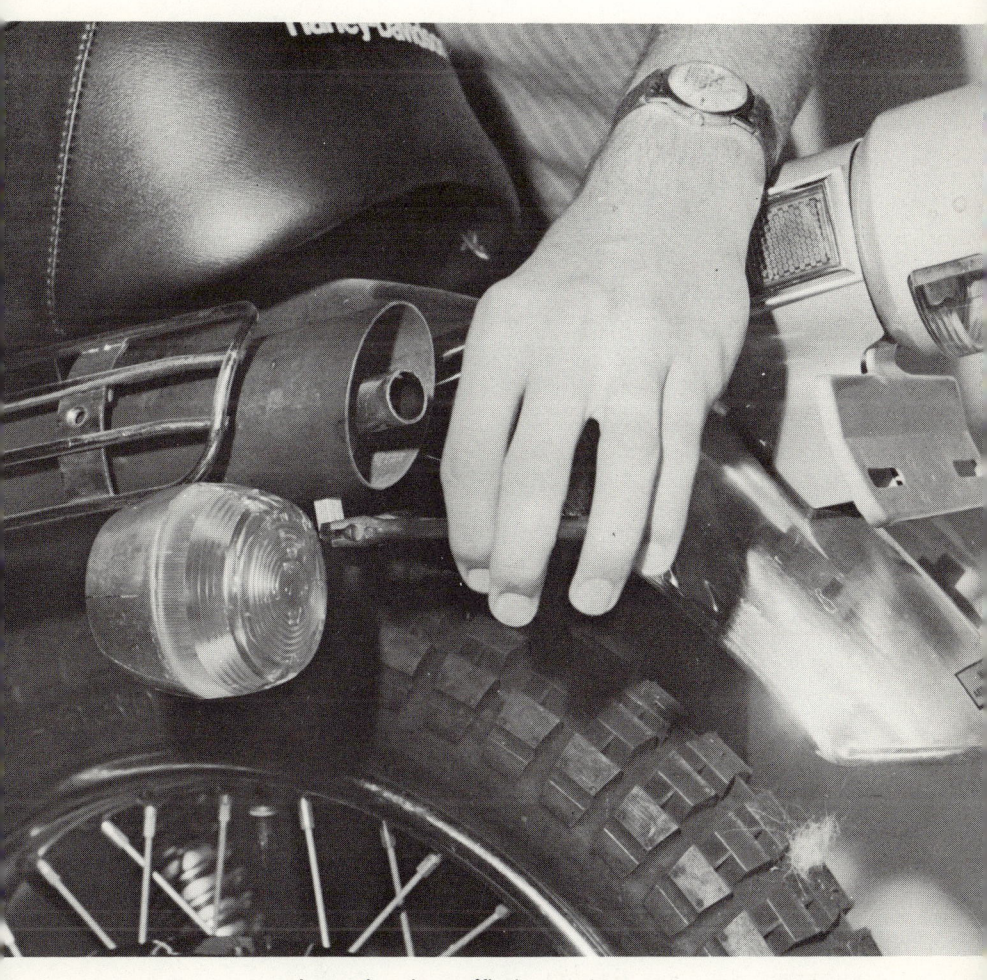
Loosening the muffler's set screw.

Checking the battery's water level.

in hot weather, you should remove the battery from your bike and service it.

First unscrew the filler plugs from the cells and add distilled water into the cells to cover the perforated strip that rests slightly above the plate separators.

Be careful not to overfill. This will only weaken the solution and splash the dangerous acid around. Overfilling can cause the cables to corrode and parts near the battery to be damaged by the acid. Be sure not to allow the acid in the battery to fall below the level of the plate separators while the rig is being used.

If a white deposit builds up on your battery terminals or battery top, wash it off with a soda-water solution. Use one-half pound of baking soda to two quarts of water. Don't get any of this highly alkaline solution inside the battery. When the alkali stops bubbling on the battery and cables, it has neutralized the acid. Now wash it off with clear water and dry all parts.

When they are dry, coat the battery terminals with heavy grease to retard corroding.

Keep your battery well charged during extremely cold weather, so the electrolyte can't separate from the water and allow the water to freeze, breaking open the casing and ruining the battery.

8 Rear drive chain

Each time your odometer reaches the 1,000-mile mark you should service your drive chain. First look for damaged or worn chain links. If you find either condition, simply replace the chain. A damaged link could produce serious problems for you including a breakdown far from aid.

If the chain is still good, begin servicing it by brushing the dirt off and wiping it down. Then work chain grease into it, or use one of the chain sprays or chain-saver lubricants.

At the 5,000-mile mark, remove the chain from the bike and inspect it carefully for wear. Take the chain off by removing the spring-locked connecting link.

Lay the chain out and clean it carefully. Lay it flat and close up the chain by taking up all the slack in its links. Measure it. Then stretch the chain out to its full length and again measure the distance. If the difference is more than one inch or if it has any stiff or damaged links, the chain should be replaced.

If the chain is in good shape, clean it thoroughly. First soak and wash completely in a pan of kerosene. Be sure to do this in the open where ventilation is good. Hang up the clean chain to dry, then lubricate as before with chain grease. Work the lubricant into the bearings by moving the chain, then wipe off all excess oil and install.

Section 2

Minor Bike Repairs

Now that you've got your hands greasy and learned more about your bike, move on to the tougher mechanical jobs. These are all easy service operations, jobs that you can do with some practice and careful attention to instructions.

Take each job in slow and easy steps, being sure of what you're doing. We suggest you buy a copy of the service manual for your brand of bike. These usually are available for your make and model at your franchised motorcycle dealer. One will cost five to seven dollars but will be a good investment.

1 Engine tune-up

The 1,000-mile service stop is a good time to take a shot at a mini engine tune-up. You need to check several items on your bike now anyway, so do a tune-up at the same time.

In the preceding section, under #4, you learned some tips on servicing spark plugs. That's your first job. Take out the plug as instructed there and make sure it is in good condition. Clean it and regap the electrode. Put back on the plug lead.

Now, remove the left crankcase cover. Here we'll look over the gap and condition of the circuit-breaker points. Be sure this is done every 2,000 miles on most bikes, but a look at 1,000 won't hurt.

Remove the cam by taking out the large hexagonal nut in the center.

Dab a touch of engine oil on the felt oiler that rides on the circuit-breaker cam.

Check the point contact surfaces. They should look clean and a dull gray but slightly rough. If the points have deep pits or badly burned areas, replace them with a new set from your dealer.

Now disconnect the spark-plug wire to prevent the engine from starting. Use your hand to turn the rotor a small amount until the circuit-breaker points are open the maximum amount. Put your .016-inch wire gauge between the points and see if there is a slight drag when pushed back and forth. If so, no adjustment is needed. If you must adjust, loosen the lock screw next to the points and move the breaker assembly with a screwdriver in the adjustment slot to the right and below the lock screw. Check with wire gauge until the spacing is correct, then tighten and recheck the gap. Whenever the breaker points are moved, you should recheck the timing as well. The best way to time your bike is with a strobe timing light at a dealership.

If you do have a timing light, check the timing. Start the bike and let it run at fast idle, then aim the flashing strobe at the marks. The alignment rotor timing mark is an "A" on top of the rotor and should line up with the crankcase vertical line above it.

If it doesn't line up, you can remove the rotor as before and loosen the three screws that hold the magneto base. Then shift the base clockwise to advance the timing or counterclockwise to retard the timing, whichever you need. The spark comes just as the ignition circuit-breaker points start opening and breaks the contact.

When the timing matches the timing light blips, retighten the screws and check to make sure the contact point gap has not been changed.

Some of the new bikes have electronic ignition systems with no contact points, which eliminates one element in your tune-ups. We expect more motorbikes to be developed with the electronic ignition. Five of the bikes now on the market with the transistorized ignition are the Suzuki motorcross racers—the TM-75, TM-100, TM-125, TM-250, and TM-400.

One of the hardest-working and most reliable parts of your bike engine is the ignition coil. What it does is step up the low magneto voltage to high voltage needed to jump the electrode at the spark plug in the engine cylinder head. It is made up of primary and secondary copper wire windings with a laminated iron core and sealed in waterproof insulation. There is no way to inspect, take apart, or repair a coil and there is no need to because they last so long. Only when you think you're having ignition troubles should you even think about it. Then there are some tests you can make, to locate troubles.

In most tune-ups on cars replacement of the condenser is a routine part of the job. Not so with your motorcycle. The condenser does not need frequent replacement. If you're having ignition trouble and think that the condenser might be the problem, replace it and see if there is an improvement. On most bikes the condenser is close by the points and magneto and held in place by one or two screws.

The ignition coil.

2 Your magneto generator

The Harley TX-125 and most new bikes these days have a magneto generator. Its job is to manufacture electricity. This is done with two coils, a set of breaker points, and a single point actuating cam and rotor assembly driven by the crankshaft. As the engine runs, a four-pole rotating magnet called the rotor turns close to a pair of laminated iron pole shoes, which carry the coils. This rotation sets up an alternating current in the coils.

In most late-model bikes this power is fed into a battery that powers the ignition system, headlights, taillights, horn, turn signals. Some systems have two sets of coils generating power for different parts of the bike.

The magneto generator on your bike should last thousands of miles with little attention. Occasional lubrication of the felt cam wiper is all that is required, as well as cleaning, adjusting, or replacing the breaker points.

If you think the magneto isn't putting out enough power, you can check it easily. When any part of your lighting system does not work, be sure to inspect the wiring first. Look to see that all connections are solid and that no wires have been cut or broken or pulled loose.

You can test the ignition by taking off the spark-plug cable and putting a short nail in it, making contact with the cap wire and extending so it lies a quarter of an inch from the engine crankcase. Don't hold the wire there or you will get a stinging shock when the engine cranks over. Now crank the engine with the starter. If a spark jumps the one-quarter inch, the trouble probably is not in the magneto generator.

If there is no spark, check the breaker points and condenser as directed before.

Testing the spark plug cable.

3 Front-fork lube

If you ride much, you'll discover that the front fork isn't responding as it did when the bike was new. Remember that on most bikes you'll see, the front fork is lubricated by the oil contained in the hydraulic shock absorbers located in each fork side. If the fork does not seem to be working correctly, or if you find that quite a bit of oil has leaked from the fork, it's high time to check your fork oil.

The best way to do this is to drain out the old oil and put in new.

Support the front handlebars of your bike so the front fork is fully extended. Then take out the upper fork bracket hex head screw plug from each side of the fork. Now put a drain pan below the front wheel to catch the oil, then unscrew the lower plugs from each fork and let the oil drain out. When the oil is gone, put the lower plugs back in. Tighten fully and put in as much oil as your owner's manual says. For the Harley TX-125 it's four and one-half ounces of Harley-Davidson Sprint fork oil in each fork. Then put the upper screw plugs in place and tighten.

4 Brake adjustments

Be sure to check your rear brake adjustment after putting on a chain or moving one. It changes your braking.

Make your rear-wheel brake adjustment by using a knurled nut that may be moved to compensate for brake-lining wear. Set the brake cable adjusting nut so the brake does not start to take effect until the foot pedal is pushed downward about a half-inch. Turn the nut farther on to tighten the brake and back it off to loosen brake. After it is adjusted,

Draining front fork oil.

Adjustment for rear-wheel brake tension.

turn the wheel to see that it is rotating freely, making sure the brake is not dragging. For larger brake adjustments use the adjusting nut and screw on the cable at the rear wheel.

Readjust the front-wheel brake as needed. When it is set correctly, the hand lever on the handlebar will move freely about one-eighth of its full movement before the brake starts to take effect. If set tighter, the brake can drag. To adjust, loosen the locknut on the control adjusting screw; turn the adjusting screw down to increase the free movement of the hand lever. When your brake is set properly, tighten the locknut securely. Major adjustment of the control cable is done by loosening the clamping block and setscrews and changing position on the cable. Minor movements can be made by loosening the locknut and turning the knurled nut located at the hand lever.

5 Tires

Removing a tire on a motorcycle is only slightly more complicated than on a bicycle. You must remove either front or rear wheels for repair or replacement of tires and tubes. For the rear wheel, you must locate and remove the chain connecting link and disengage the chain from the rear sprocket. Remove the brake adjusting nut and disconnect the brake cable. Remove the rear axle nut and withdraw the axle from the left side of motorcycle to allow removal of the wheel from the fork axle clips. Engage the brake side plate in the fork anchor stud on the right fork side. Your wheel bearings should be replaced at each 5,000-mile interval. If your bike gets submerged in water, the bearings should be repacked at once. Use special bearing grease as directed in your owner's manual.

Be sure to keep your tires properly inflated. Again check your owner's manual. On the Harley TX-125, for example, both front and rear tires should be kept at 18 pounds per square inch. That's for a 150-pound rider. For each extra 50 pounds of rider you increase pressure by two pounds in back and one pound in front. Don't be surprised if the front tire on your bike wears unevenly. This is simply the nature of the machine we call a motorcycle. Be sure to inspect your tires each 2,000 miles. Look for tread wear, cuts, snags, punctures. Check your pressure with your own tested tire gauge every Monday morning before the bike has been ridden.

6 Adjusting the headlight

The headlamps on most motorcycles today are sealed-beam units. When your light burns or jolts out of operation, be sure to replace it with exactly the same type, size, and voltage that was in the light previously.

The sealed-beam unit is simple to remove. Take off the outer molding screw beneath the headlamp housing. Pull the sealed-beam unit and gasket out of the rubber molding. Now take the connector block from the sealed-beam unit prongs.

Install the new sealed-beam unit by reversing this process. Place the unit so it registers correctly with the gasket and housing. Make sure the connector block contacts are clean to ensure a good electrical contact.

Check now to be sure the light is aimed correctly. Move your bike 25 feet from a wall on a flat area and mark the center of the beam of light on the wall. Have the bike resting on both wheels and in straight-ahead alignment. Now sit on the bike as you would when riding so the front fork will compress naturally. The top of the main beam of light should register on the wall even with the line you drew even with the sealed-beam center. Make adjustments with the headlamp mounting stud underneath the lower fork bracket.

Outer molding screw on headlight.

7 Changing the oil

In this Harley always use two-cycle oil. Check the oil level every month or after each 1,000 miles, whichever comes first. Doing this is simple. Remove the oil level plug on the transmission and add oil through the transmission filler plug hole until oil overflows from the plug opening.

Of course, be sure that your bike is standing straight up when you check and add oil to the transmission.

When your mileage indicator shows that you have had 5,000 miles' worth of fun from your bike, it's time to drain and refill your transmission. If you don't ride 5,000 miles a year, drain the transmission at the end of your first year with the bike. The best way to dispose of oil in the city is to empty it into a large plastic jug, such as a detergent or bleach jug, cap it tightly, and then put it in your garbage can.

Some filling stations have oil sumps where you can drain out your oil. Be sure to ask the station owner if you can do this. Usually they won't care, since they sell the oil for reprocessing later.

If you're making a cross-country run and your transmission gets submerged in water, drain it as soon as possible and refill to the correct level with two-cycle oil.

Section 3

Trouble-Fixing Your Bike

Most motorcycles are simple and efficient machines. They start easily, run well, and are remarkably trouble-free. However, when your bike won't start, won't run right, loses power, or some other problem crops up that stops you from enjoying your wheels, it's an immediate crisis.

The best way to tackle problems is to know enough so you yourself can check it. If the spark-plug wire got knocked off, for instance, it would be a waste of time and money to haul your bike back to the dealer. On the other hand, if you've got a heavy knocking noise from the bottom end of your engine during acceleration, you know either the

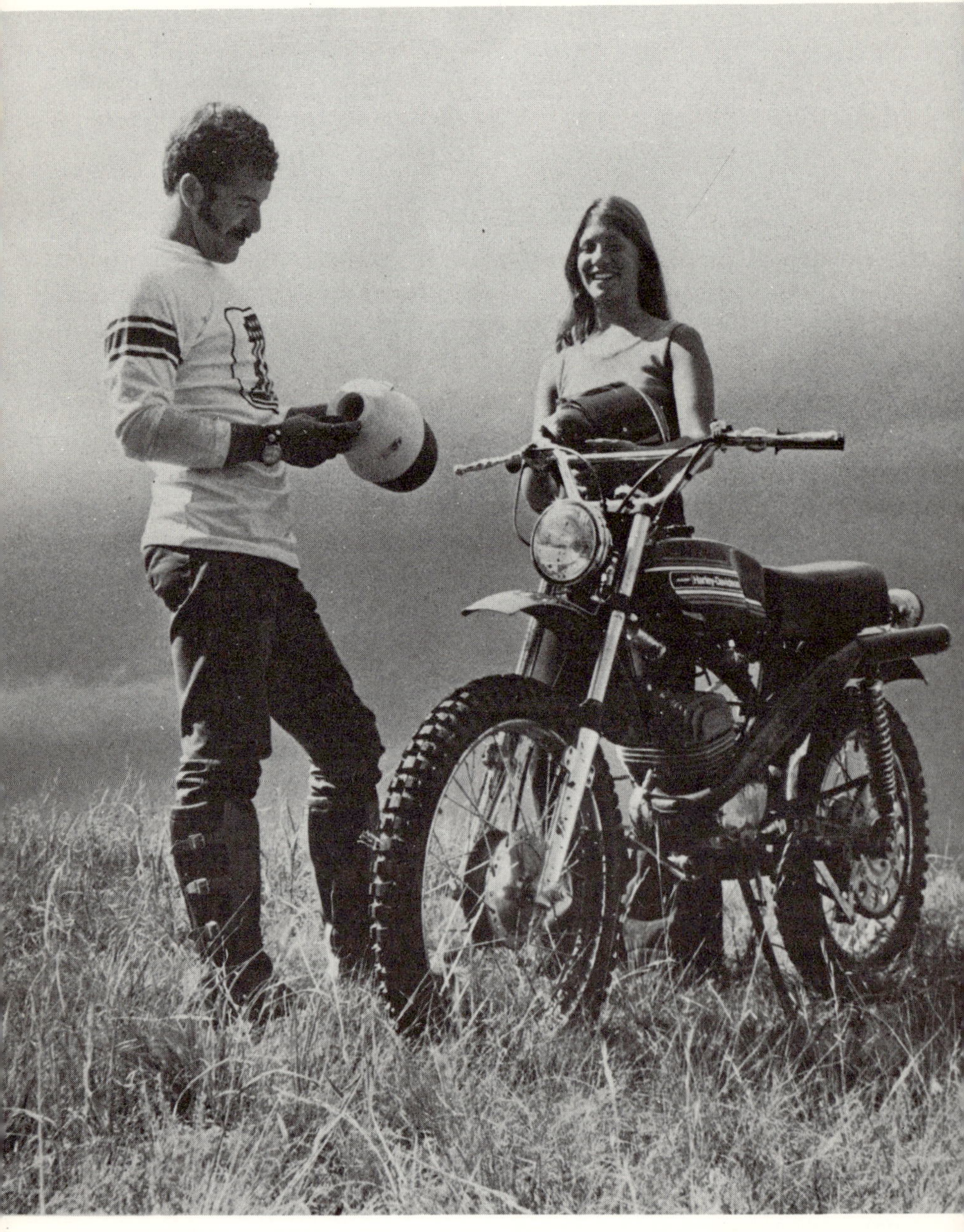

bearings or the crankshaft is in deep trouble and you better get some expert mechanical help.

There are probably a hundred little checks you can make on your bike when something goes wrong. "Trouble-fixing" your bike is what it's all about, and this section is designed to help you save money and have more fun and enjoyment. The more you know now about a bike, the easier it's going to be to persuade your folks to help you buy one—when the right time comes.

This trouble-fixing section is cut up into several divisions, each aimed at checking a different part of the motorcycle. Generally you will find three big areas of trouble with your bike: one is the ignition system, the second is the fuel system, and the third is centered around problems of compression.

You need all three of these elements to make your engine run: fuel, spark, and compression. First let's talk about what to do:

1 If your engine won't start

1. First check to be sure the key is in "on" position and that the fuel-supply valve is turned on. Your transmission must also be in neutral position for the engine to start.

2. Open the fuel tank and determine the amount of gasoline. Sometimes a low fuel level will make starting difficult. Fill the tank to the maximum if this problem continues.

3. If all seems to be normal but you still can't get the engine to fire, your fuel line may be plugged. Disconnect and "blow it out" to be sure it is clear. Reassemble and try again.

4. In some cases a low or discharged battery will prevent your cycle from starting. Check for spark at the plug as outlined in the previous section in #2. If you have no spark, check the electrolyte level in the battery and recharge your battery if needed.

Wet fouling of spark plug.

5. Repeated spraying of fuel into a piston that doesn't fire will soon wet-foul your spark plug. If this happens, you can say the engine is "flooded." Remove the spark plug, dry it off with a cloth or blow it dry with compressed air. You might also clean it at a filling station with an air-operated cleaner and abrasive. Reinstall the plug and try to start your bike again.

6. Flooded engine due to fuel-supply valve left in "on" position when bike was not being used. Turn the valve to "off" setting and dry plug as in tip #5.

7. Repeated unsuccessful attempts to start your cycle may mean the contact breaker points or ignition timing is out of adjustment. Correct as suggested in the tune-up section of this book, or have a dealership retune and check your ignition system.

8. A defective ignition coil or condenser will also prevent the cycle from starting. Check these units and replace them as needed.

9. A run-down battery and lack of spark from your system could be the result of a defective magneto generator. Check that section for suggestions how to correct this situation.

10. Lack of spark to your plug could be the result of a poorly seated plug lead or boot. Check to be sure wire is attached firmly to plug top and that the lead is secure on the other end.

11. Check the battery terminals. If they are fouled or corroded, broken or simply loosely connected, not enough juice will get through to fire your engine.

12. Spark plug. Examine plug for proper spark gap, for fouling of any sort as suggested in section on spark plugs.

13. Lack of spark can sometimes be the result of other loose wires in the ignition circuit. Check all wiring to be sure it is tight and properly connected.

14. In some cases lack of ability to start the engine is due to the clutch slipping and not turning the engine over so it can start. Better see a dealer for this one.

15. Fouled contact points. As points are used, they tend to pit and build up, or foul themselves. This can lead to lack of starting power. Check yours and clean or replace as needed.

16. On many bikes fuel and oil are mixed. (This is not so on the Harley-Davidson TX-125 and many other later-model bikes.) Check to be sure your mixture is right, or simply drain the fuel from the tank, remix it in the correct proportions, and fill your tank. Kick over the engine several times to get the new fuel into the carburetor and give it a good try.

17. Valves that stick or are simply too tight can often cause your machine to refuse to start. Again this is a more technical problem, and if you find nothing else the matter, go see your franchised dealer for his aid and comfort.

18. If you have driven your bike cross country during the winter, you may find that your heavier engine and transmission oil for California is not at all suited to Denver, Minneapolis, or New York in winter-

time. You'll need to drain the oil and replace with one of lighter consistency.

19. If your engine is hard to start, the battery may be so low that it is barely able to crank the engine over. For this one, ride enough to charge up the battery or have it recharged at a filling station or dealership.

20. A carburetor out of adjustment can also make your rig hard to start. Mark this down to have fixed on that trip to your dealership.

21. Hard starting may also indicate spark-plug cable fitting loosely and leaking power; wires loosely connected at battery, coil, and breaker points; oil that is too heavy for winter riding. Solutions here are easy to take care of.

2 Other engine trouble-fixing problems

22. If your engine is using too much oil (on models with separate oil tank), it could indicate one of several problems. Your piston rings might be worn or frozen. Your valve guides could be badly worn or you might simply have an oil leak to the outside of the engine through a tube, pipe, or filler. The other possibility is that your engine oil grade might be too light. If all else fails, try a step heavier in the oil weight.

23. Engine idles poorly and sometimes misfires during acceleration. This might result from incorrect carburetor adjustment. Dirty, fouled, or improperly gapped spark plugs could do it too; check these. Look at your spark-plug cable for a poor connection.

24. If your engine backfires or the kick starter kicks back on you, it could be that your ignition timing is too far **advanced**, or that your automatic advance unit is sticking in the forward position on your contact breaker.

25. Some engines will make spark plugs foul repeatedly and with no apparent cause. But there is a cause. Check these: Your engine may be simply idling too long, letting the plug load up from cool running. The plug might be too cold a plug for your type of riding. Check it with your dealer. Your fuel mixture may be too rich, allowing oil fouling of the plug.

26. Loss of power. This almost always means a loss of engine compression. Some of the causes can be: valves sticking because of gummy stems, collapsed or damaged piston, badly worn piston rings, a leaking or blown head gasket, or the exhaust ports or muffler may be clogged with carbon on two-stroke engines. The easiest solution to this problem is to clean a clogged air cleaner, but usually it's more serious.

27. If your engine overheats: The valves or rings may be excessively worn. Or you may have an oil-supply problem because oil helps cool an engine. Your oil supply may not be adequate or circulating properly or the pump's not working hard enough. Carbon may be the culprit. It can cling to the piston crown, stop up the muffler or the exhaust port. Your ignition timing may be retarded too far or the automatic advance unit sticking in the retarded position.

28. If your engine idles poorly or misfires during acceleration it could be: defective ignition coil or condenser or a weak spark. A bad spark-plug cable could do it. Also check the ignition timing, the movement of the automatic advance unit, and air leakage at the carburetor manifold. In some cases water in your fuel will give this effect, as will the plugging of the gas tank cap vent. A weak or broken valve spring is another outside chance here.

29. Engine slows after sustained high speed operation. For this problem check your spark plug. It may be too hot a plug and cause preignition. In extreme cases the piston could be seriously overheating and about ready to seize. More likely the carburetor mixture is too lean, causing the machine to run hot. As a last resort, check for poor oil supply. The oil may not be circulating or the pump may be failing to help cool interior parts.

30. Engine detonation or preignition. Look at the plug and see if it is correct for your use. It probably is too hot, so go a step lower in plug heat range. The ignition timing is usually too far advanced. It could be insufficient oil mixed with the fuel or injected into fuel by the mixing mechanism. Your carburetor mixture could be too lean or the fuel octane rating too low. Again, carbon deposits on the piston crown or exhaust port to the muffler could do it. You might also check for an air leak at the carburetor manifold.

3 Carburetor trouble-fixing ideas

31. If your idle mixture is too rich, it could be due to dirt or other "foreign" matter in the idle channel. Blowing the channel clear should fix that. It can mean that the intermediate needle is adjusted too lean, that the welch plug or channel plugs are missing or leaking, or that the nozzle check valve is not seating. Your dealer can help here.

32. If your bike leans out too much at sustained high speeds it may mean: Dirt is in the nozzle system, so blow it clear. It might be that the main jet is too small, damaged, or blocked or that the main jet plug screw is not secured.

33. If your carburetor floods repeatedly, check these: Your float probably is set too high. Reposition it as detailed in your manual. The fuel inlet valve could be sticking. The inlet valve or the valve seat might be worn or damaged. Or there might be dirt between the valve and its seat. Also check to see if the carburetor float is sticking due to improper alignment in the bowl. And finally check to see that the inlet lever on the carburetor is properly set. Of course, it can always be the fuel-control valve left open when the machine is not in operation. Always turn it off after riding.

34. If you get a lean mixture at sustained midrange speeds, check:

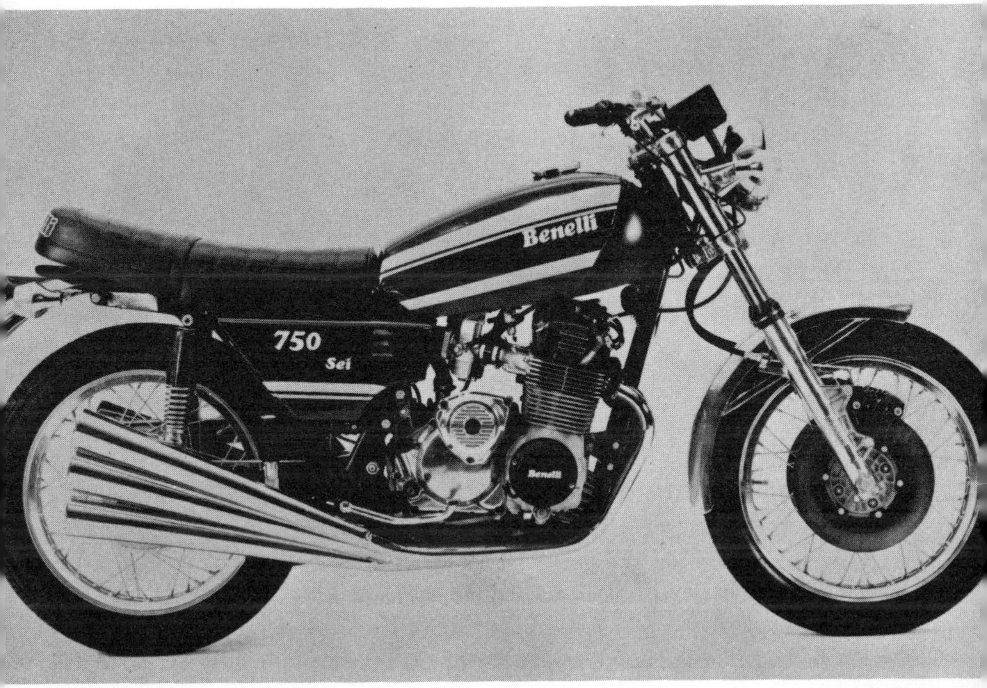
Benelli
750
Sei
Benelli

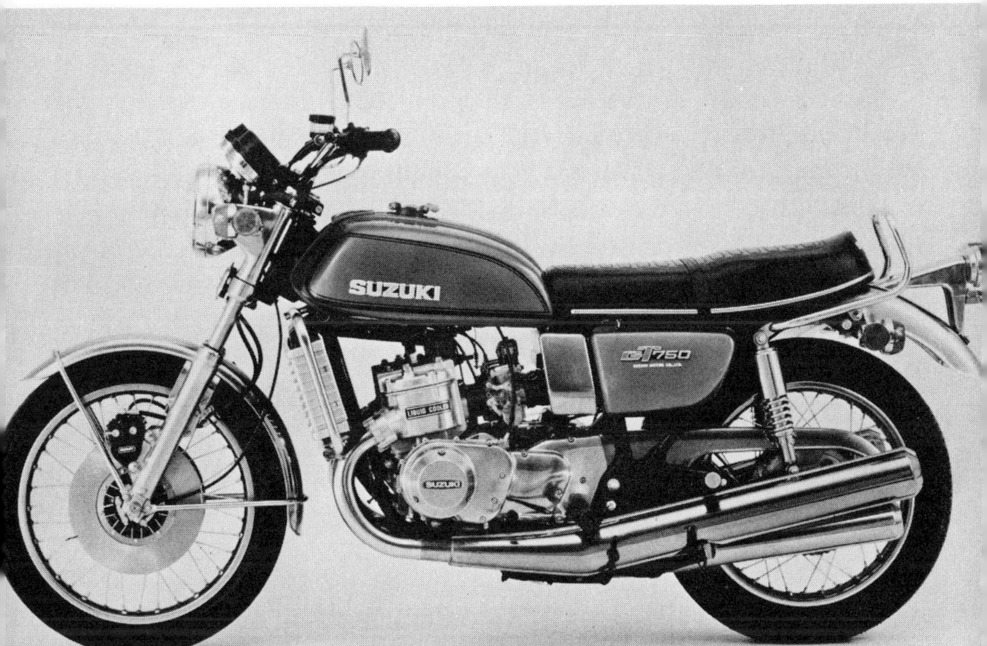
SUZUKI
GT750
LIQUID COOLED
SUZUKI

The intermediate adjustment may be too lean; adjust. Again, dirt is probably in the fuel ports or channels. The welch plugs or channel plugs could be missing or leaking, or the nozzle check valve is not seating. Also look for the intermediate adjustment packing to see if it is missing or damaged.

35. But what if your idle mixture is too lean? Probably your carburetor is flooding. If not, the idle adjustment screw may be blunted; if so, replace it. The idle adjustment hole could be damaged or oversized.

36. If you have a rich mixture throughout the throttle range, it could be carburetor flooding again. Or your choke might be improperly adjusted.

37. If the rich mixture shows only at sustained high speeds, the answer probably is that the main jet is too large or loose. If not, the carburetor is probably flooded.

38. A rich mixture at sustained midrange speeds has the same causes, usually as in #37 plus: The nozzle check valve welch plug is probably loose. Or the choke is not adjusted correctly, or the intermediate jet adjustment is set too rich.

39. A lean mixture during the whole speed range can mean the filter screens are plugged or dirty. It might be the inlet lever positioned wrong or an air leak in the metering system or at the manifold.

40. If the lean mixture shows during acceleration, check for dirt in the fuel channels and improper carburetor adjustment, and look to see if the accelerator pump has been damaged or worn.

4 Driveline trouble-fixing

This is an ultracomplicated part of your bike. No one without an excellent mechanical sense, ability, and training should dig around in

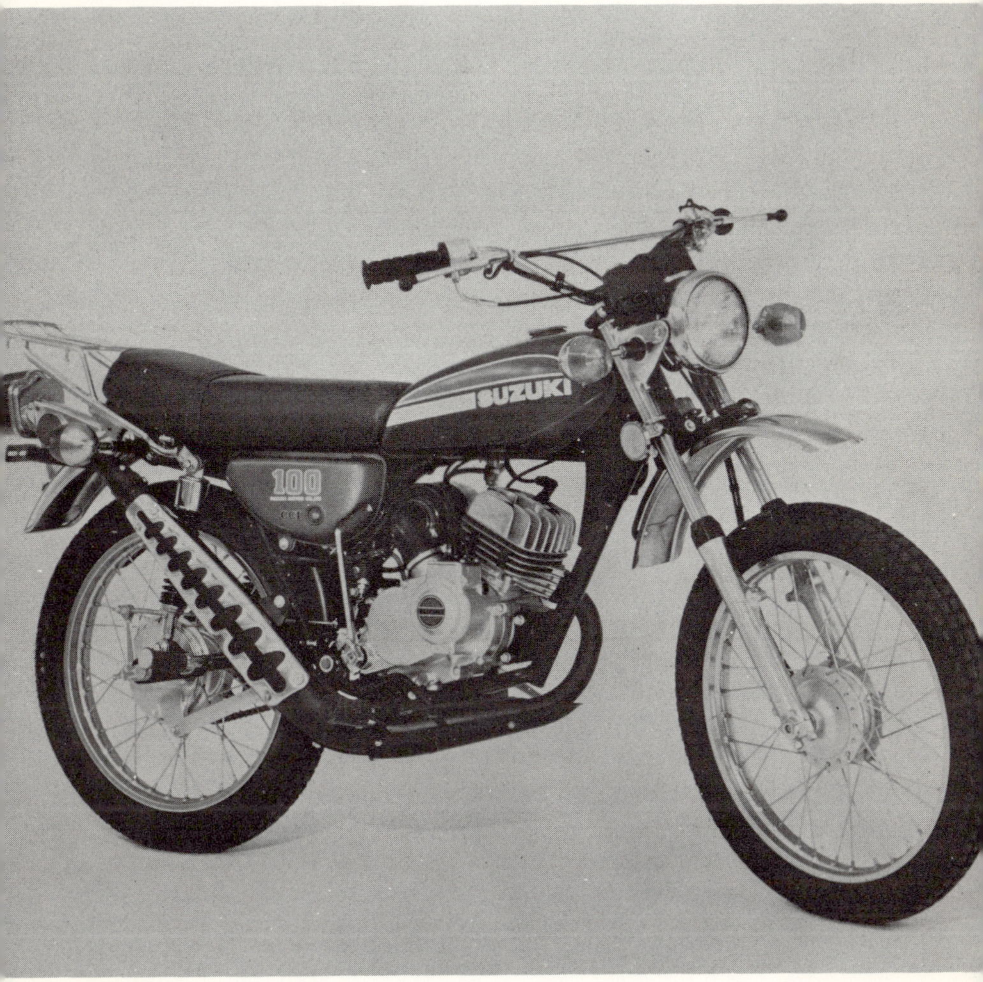
SUZUKI
100

this part of a bike. But there are some signs that you can watch for and we'll give some suggestions of what might be wrong.

41. If your clutch chatters it could be due to the clutch disc rivets being loose. The clutch spring disc could be excessively flattened.

42. If your clutch slips: The release mechanism probably is adjusted incorrectly. The friction discs could be worn or soaked with oil. The clutch spring tension might be too loose, or the release worm and lever may be sticking.

43. When your clutch drags: The release lever and worm are excessively worn. Or the clutch spring tension might be too loose, or the release worm and lever may be sticking.

44. Another clutch problem: The clutch spring tension is too tight. Maybe the release mechanism is incorrectly adjusted. Your friction discs

could be gummy. Or the steel plates may be warped. The clutch sprocket keys may be excessively worn or damaged.

45. If your transmission jumps out of gear, it could be due to improperly adjusted shifter rods or the shifter forks out of kilter. Insufficient spring tension could do it or a worn gear dog or cam plate.

46. If the transmission shifts hard, it could be due to the clutch dragging, too heavy transmission oil, bent shifter rods, or shifter forks bent by excessive force used when shifting.

47. If your clutch grinds when shifting into first gear, check to see if the transmission oil is too heavy.

48. If the kick starter acts up by sticking after a starting stroke, or if the starter lever slips during a starting stroke, or if the starter lever remains in the down position, it probably means the starter spring is broken.

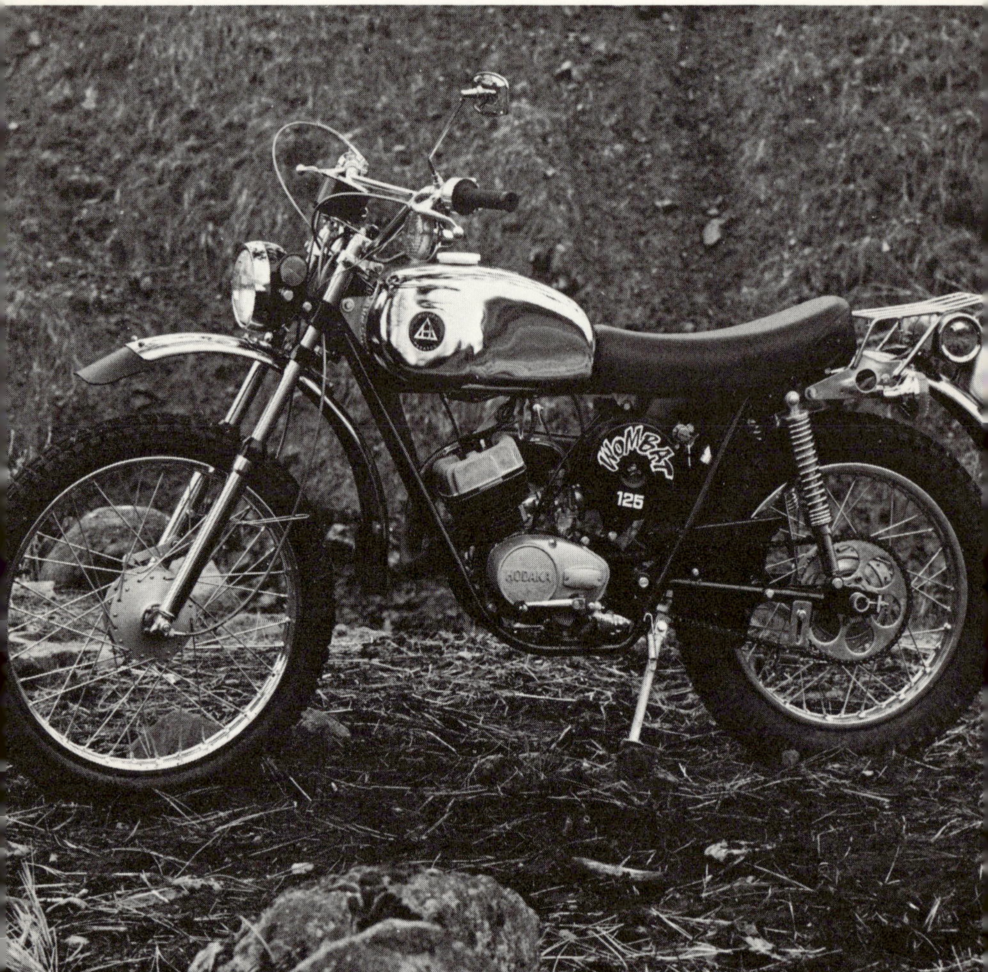
WOMBAT
125

5 Trouble-fixing the frame

49. Engine vibration: Look at the cylinder head bracket to see if it's loose or broken; if so, secure or replace. The engine mounting bolts might be loose or your frame broken. Your primary chain might be badly worn, too tight, or not lubricated well enough.

50. Excessive chain noise: If the chain slaps due to too much play, adjust it as explained in your owner's manual. Not a tough job. If it whines due to being too tight, loosen it a little.

51. Wheel vibrations: You could have loose spokes; secure them and tighten according to specifications. A wheel rim out of true can cause vibration. Get it back in shape. A loose axle nut can cause problems. Tighten it; check others. Your rear wheel could be out of alignment. Set it right with the line of the front wheel. Unevenly worn tires cause noise. Replace the tires and check your alignment. Even underinflation can cause problems. Keep tire pressure to suggested levels. Excessive front-end loading can cause problems. End them by removing some of the weight from the front wheel.

52. Poor front fork operation: This may mean you're low on oil or that the fork oil is contaminated. Replace it and check operation again. The fork may have worn or leaky seals that caused contaminated oil. Replace them. The trouble could also be a worn breather valve, a worn shock absorber or collapsed spring, excessive clearance in slider bushings. Bent tubes, stem, brackets, or sliders could be the culprits as well.

53. If your brakes do not function well: It could be that the cause is glazed or worn brake pads. The pads may be oil- or grease-soaked or the linkage improperly adjusted.

6 Trouble-fixing the electrical system

54. Your generator seems to be charging below normal. It probably is a wrongly adjusted voltage regulator. But it could be a loose coil terminal or broken field coil wire. It might be worn commutators or the brushes could be sticking in the holders. The armature might be defective. See your dealer.

55. If your contact points burn or pit rapidly, you can bet it's a defective condenser. Replace it and see the difference. If that doesn't solve the problem, check the condenser terminals. They should be securely fastened. Remember, dirty contact points will pit. Be sure not to touch the faces with your fingers.

56. If your magneto generator doesn't charge, look for a deenergized magneto rotor or a grounded, open, or shorted coil.

57. If the generator does not charge, check the brushes. They may be worn or stuck. It might also be an improperly grounded voltage regulator or one worn out. There are other possibilities: dirty or oily commutator, grounded generator terminal, loose or broken lead in the battery generator circuit, shorted commutator, a bad armature, grounded positive brush holder, a loose coil terminal or broken field coil wire, or cut-out points not closing.

Remember, trouble-fixing is fine on your bike, just as long as you know what you are doing. The second you get in over your head, you are liable to cause more trouble than was there in the first place.

If you don't know what to do and how to do it, leave the problem to the experts. If you are serious about knowing all about your bike and what makes it tick, buy a service manual.

Several independent publishers put out service manuals for motorcycles, including Chilton Book Company. They have a clothbound

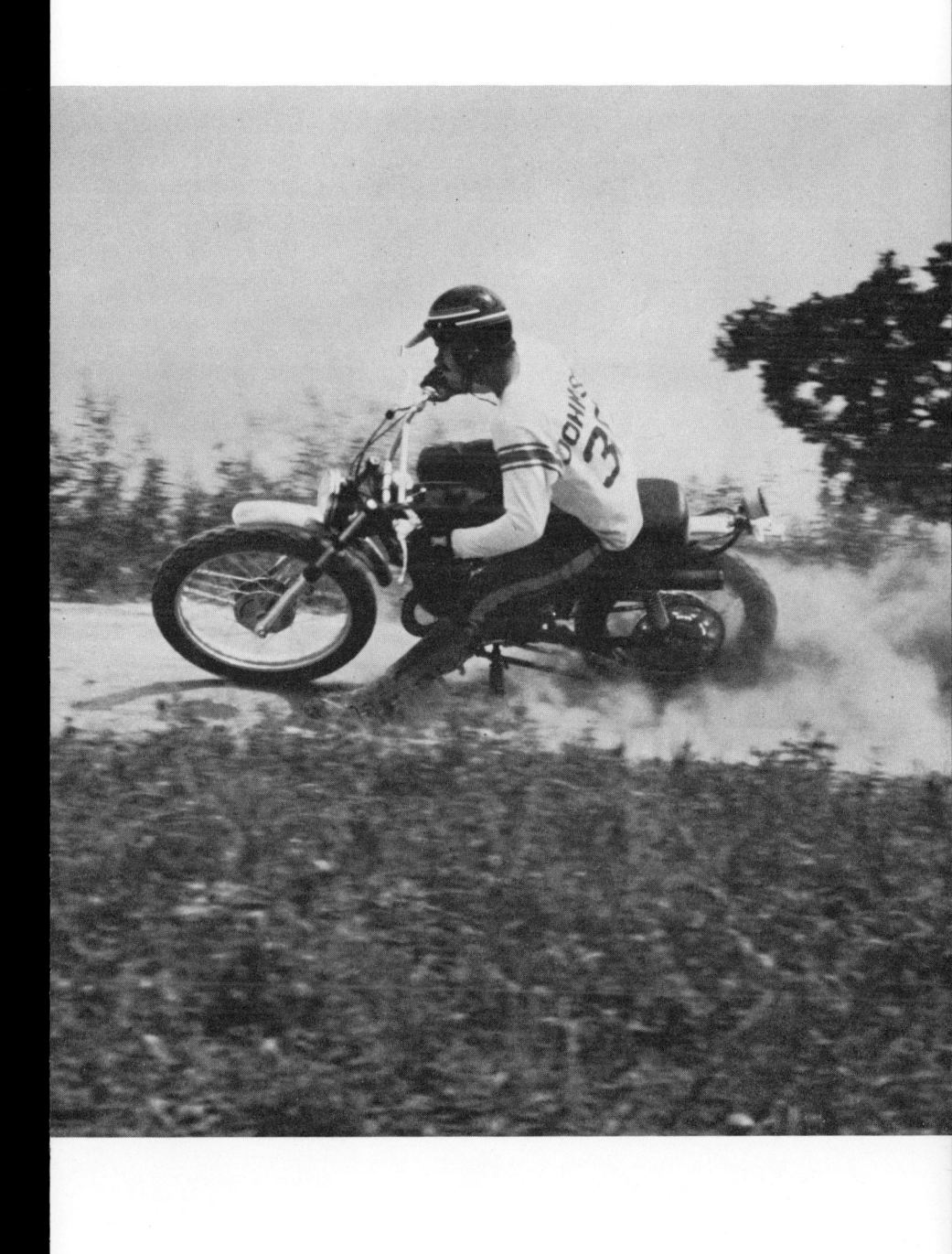

book called *Harley-Davidson Singles*. One came out in 1973 and these are issued frequently to keep up with new models.

Another big producer of repair and service handbooks is Clymer Publications in Los Angeles. They have service-repair handbooks for most popular motorcycles and issue them on a frequent basis to keep up with new products.

7   Some questions about your bike

Following are some of the questions most often asked about a motorcycle and ones that we have not covered elsewhere in the general maintenance sections.

1. *How should I store my bike for a short time?* It's best to store your bike in a clean, dry place, heated if possible in winter. Here are some storage procedures.

Clean it up first, with a good washing. Then ride it until it's up to normal operating temperature and all motor and chassis parts are completely dry.

Check the oil level and fill it to the full mark. Also fill the fuel tank to the top with your regular fuel, mixed or straight, whichever your bike takes.

Check the battery electrolyte level and add water if needed. Charge the battery if needed to bring it to full power. Disconnect the positive lead, clean the battery top completely, and then coat the terminals with heavy grease or petroleum jelly such as Vaseline.

Lubricate the bike completely at all grease fittings.

Wax and polish all painted and chrome surfaces. An extraheavy coating of wax will help protect the surfaces during storage.

Place your bike on a center stand or kick stand or block it upright. You may wish to rest tires on wood if storage is to be for a long period, since concrete can lead to tire deterioration.

Cover your bike with an old blanket or sleeping bag. If you store it outside, use a heavy plastic cover. Once a month or so wipe it down to help prevent rusting.

2. *Will water hurt the engine when I'm washing my bike?* Probably not. Remember to cover your air cleaner and spark-plug lead before washing so they don't get soaked. Don't spray the carburetor and wheel bearings with a commercial car-wash detergent. When you have it dried off, ride it for about ten minutes to get the engine entirely dry. If it won't start, some part of the ignition circuit is probably wet. Dry off vital parts and try again. If it still won't start, let it sit an hour and try again.

3. *Is it all right to paint the engine, the cylinder, and head?* The thin,

liquid paint is fine, since it does not retain heat inside the engine. Metallic paint or aluminum paint should never be used on cylinders or heads since they hold the heat in the cylinder, which can seriously overheat your bike and cause expensive problems.

4. *Can I "jump" start my bike, as is done on cars with a dead battery?* Yes. Do it this way: Cross the handlebars with another bike so they are grounded together. Then put a jump wire from the charged battery to the spark coil terminal, the one that goes to the switch wire. Now hit your kick starter and you should have power to start. Once started, the generator should begin charging up your dead or low battery.

5. *Can I use commercial "Gunk" on my engine? Will it strip off the paint?* Yes and no. Most "Gunk"-type degreasers work very well on built-up grease and oil on an engine. But if you get it on the painted parts or let it stay on them very long, you're bound to lose some paint. "Gunk" is especially tough on painted plastics. A good washing with detergent and hot water will usually do an effective job. Then rinse, dry, and use a good liquid or paste auto wax on the chrome and the painted parts for a long-lasting wash job.

6. *Is it true that you shouldn't add water to your battery in subfreezing weather?* No, the battery must have water. If you need to add quite a bit, add it just before you go for a ride. That way the electrolyte will have a chance to mix completely with the new water. The mixture does not freeze easily, but plain water unmixed would freeze a little under 32°F.

7. *Won't softer, underinflated tires give me an easier, softer ride?* True, but they also wear out faster and could lead to a sidewall blowout. On a fast corner your front tire could roll right off the rim! Put your best tire on the front and keep it properly inflated. Overinflation makes for a hard ride, can lead to impact blowouts, and makes your front end hard to control.

8. *If I don't run my bike in the winter, do I need to protect the bat-*

tery? You bet. If you won't be running your bike for two months or more, take the battery out of it and give it a full charge, then store in a dry, clean location that does not freeze, but doesn't get over 110°F. Every month look in the battery and add distilled water to bring the cells up full. Then charge it for five hours at one-ampere rate.

9. *Why do bike gas caps have holes in them?* The holes are there to avoid creating a back pressure in the tank. As the gas runs out, air must be let into the tank to replace it. If the tank were sealed tightly, gas would not feed into the carburetor as needed, and the engine would be starved for fuel, sputter, and die.

10. *Can I take my bike down to the corner filling station to have the battery charged?* Yes, but be careful. Tell the man that it should not be charged at a rate of over two amperes, and taper it off to one ampere as the battery comes to full charge. A high rate charger as used on a car or a "fast charge" can seriously damage and might ruin a motorcycle battery.

8 Mini tips for the care and riding of your bike

Hints for longer bike tire wear. Start slowly; don't burn rubber off your tires. Stop slowly; don't grind them down. Corner moderately. A fast corner can burn off a hundred miles of steady-driving rubber. Lower your speed on a rough road and for sharp chuckholes. Drive at moderate speeds in hotter weather.

*During cold weather the air pressur*e in your bike tires will decrease, so be sure to check your tires every two weeks and bring the pressure up to the proper level. Do this before riding in the morning or as soon as you get to the first filling station, or use your pocket pressure gauge before starting. Then add the number of pounds of pressure you're low when you get to the station.

On expressways and freeways move to the right-hand lane at least a mile before you come to your off-ramp. This eliminates any last-minute lane cutting, horn honking, and angry looks.

Keep your eyes moving when you ride. Work them up and down and side to side so you know what's in front of you, behind, and to each side. Check behind before making any turn or lane change. Know what's there. Always double-check at a stoplight to be sure no one is charging through it.

Put up a cardboard chart on your garage wall or in your room. List the regular maintenance jobs—oil change, lube, oil filter, air cleaner. Beside each item put the mileage figure indicating when the work should be done again. A quick look at the board and your mileage indicator tells you what you need to do next. For that next cross-country trip cut your road map into convenient parts about four by nine inches. Number them in the order you'll need them, and keep handy for inflight reading.

Always anticipate the movements of cars. Watch the left front wheel. This wheel telegraphs the movements of a car, especially one stopped at a light or coming in from a cross street. The wheel usually is turned by the driver before the car begins to move.

Keep a small pill bottle full of dimes in one of your saddlebags or your tool kit. They come in handy for telephone calls or parking meters —especially when you've run out of pocket change.

Accelerate before passing a car or truck. You should be moving fifteen miles per hour faster than the car you are passing. This allows you to get around and back into your lane quickly. Especially true on directly opposed, two-lane roads.

Best way to ride a curve: Slow down before you enter the curve. During the turn, keep your throttle on and speed up slightly as you come out of it. The power-on gives your rear wheel more traction to overcome the centrifugal force, helping you corner more safely.

Enjoying a bay.

Exploring a cave.

Is it more economical to let your engine idle for two or three minutes or shut it off and start it? It is much more gas saving to turn off an idling engine. It's a waste of gasoline to idle it more than thirty seconds.

Always carry one red fusee-type of railroad flare in your saddlebag or even taped to the frame or under the seat. It's very handy if you have a slight crash—or to give to some four-wheeler who has.

It's easier to work at night with a flashlight if you tape or tie the light to the inside of your wrist so it shines at the palm of your hand. Keep two heavy rubber bands around a flashlight for that emergency.

If you keep distilled battery water at home, try putting it in a thoroughly washed-out detergent bottle. The water can be squirted out the top and directly into your battery with no spillage.

If your turn signals are blinking too rapidly, it may be that one of the bulbs is burned out. Replace the defective bulb and this should restore the indicator to its normal blinking frequency.

If you have a partly opened can of engine, transmission, or fork oil on your bench, keep it dust-free by putting a slightly larger-diameter can upside down over the oil can. Then try to remember what you've hidden!

Remember that bicycle riders are not pedestrians; in most states bicycles are considered "vehicles" and must obey the traffic laws. That means you must give them right of way, position on the roadway, and other courtesies you would another motorcycle or car.

Sometimes you'll find an impossible place where you must start a bolt or screw and there's only room for one hand. Try dripping candle wax into the head slot of the screw or bolt, then force your screwdriver into the hardened wax. The screw will stay on the end of your tool the way a magnetized screw would.

Horns are going up in pitch. Psychologists tell us that a high-pitched horn has a greater effective warning distance. The higher-pitched tone also takes less energy from your cycle battery.

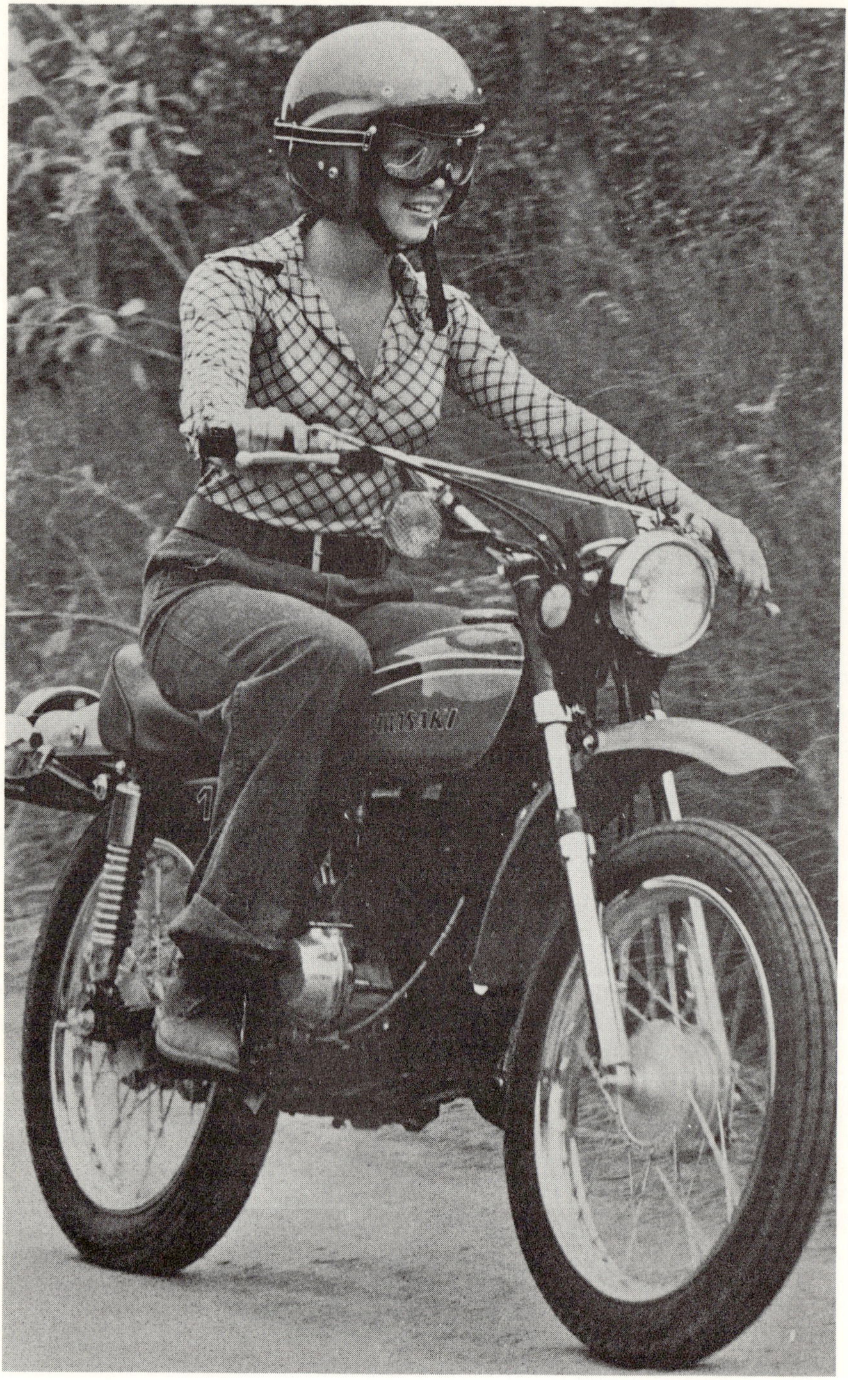

When riding a freeway or open road on your bike, it may seem that you're going much slower than you actually are. Believe your speedometer. You may be going too fast for a turnoff or a sudden corner. Remember, speed on a flat surface seems as much as 50 percent below real velocity.

If you ever hallucinate when riding, see strange shapes, colors, trucks, or trees that aren't there—stop and get off the road at once. If you're alone, take a nap or sleep the rest of the night or day. Hallucinations often come from exhaustion after long, nonstop riding jaunts.

One good way to blow dirt out of the spark-plug well on your bike before removing the plug is to use an empty plastic detergent bottle with the nozzle snipped off. Squeeze the bottle sharply and a jet of air shoots out, blowing away the debris.

After riding past a car or another bike, it's a good rule of thumb not to cut back into that lane until you can see the other rig in your rearview mirror, if you have one. If not, look back over your shoulder to be sure you have lots of clearance.

Section 4

Accessories and Improvements

When you start riding, you'll begin thinking about ways to customize your bike to make it fit your personality.

One way is to make your own "chopper" or extended bike, with loads of chrome parts, a long front fork, sissy bar in back, and a wild seat. The only problem is that many of these choppers cost as much as five thousand dollars. Besides some questions about their safety, we've eliminated the chopper as a possibility for your customizing jobs because of cost.

In changing your bike, remember that your street bike is carefully manufactured to meet government standards. The bike is "streetable,"

A custom paint job.

meaning it has the turn signals, side lights, muffler, and other required mechanical gear to bring it into compliance with all motor vehicle and motorcycle regulations in effect when that particular bike was sold. You should not alter the muffler in any way—don't take it off, don't poke holes in it, don't cut off the end of it.

For most of us, customizing a bike means putting on two items: paint and accessories. With paint there is such a small surface to use that the job must be delicately done and with flair.

This forces many of us to custom painting shops, where they can do anything you want. The largest spaces for customized painting are the bike's tank, and some of the fairing or saddlebags. Wild colors and designs can be developed with one theme followed all the way through from front fender, tanks, saddle, to the rear taillight. Try it; see what you can work out—on paper first, then try it with paint. It really helps here if you're an artist or have an artist friend.

The second way to customize your bike is with accessories and "hang-ons." These might include things for your bike itself, front fairings, saddlebags on the rear, or equipment for the rider. Let's take a look at a few of these.

Most of the fairings like the one pictured here look a lot alike. They consist of a shield to protect the rider from the wind—usually heavy Plexiglas and fiberglass that extends outward to cover the handlebars, shielding the rider from rocks and rain and other minor road hazards. Fairings are ideal for the longer ride when harsh winds and heavy rains are possible. A good fairing will cut through the wind without your body absorbing the punishment, and allow you to get to your destination more relaxed. The headlight rings are usually chrome and designed to fit many different makes of motorcycles. Most mount easily with simple hand tools. You can put a fairing on yourself.

Saddlebags. There are a great many types and styles of equipment designed to help you carry things on a motorcycle. Most common is the saddlebag, which usually fits over the rear fender and hangs down on each side. Some of these are now solidly mounted and made of metal or fiberglass, resembling boxes more than they do bags.

How much you carry will determine the type of device for you. Most

A fairing.

bikes have no saddlebags. Some are so loaded down they look like they are kitchen-sink camping. There is even one device that straps in front of the rider directly on top of the gasoline tank. This is a soft bag type of container handy for small items and comes with a full zipper and lock. It's about a foot long, nine inches high and five deep.

Some of these, like the saddlebag trunk, are big enough to hold a sleeping bag or two crash helmets. Remember on any hang-on device such as this, you will add considerable weight when it is filled. It will change the handling of the machine, so you should accustom yourself to it.

Another approach to traveling with gear on a bike is to use some kind of pack system. You've seen the sissy bars jutting up from the back of a chopper. These look much the same, only the bars are steel frames with solid mountings and designed to have packsacks and sleeping bags strapped onto them. Most come as sets with packsack and mounting frame. Some are built short, twelve to fourteen inches high. Others extend a full two feet over the rear seat, allowing plenty of room for a full-sized camping pack and sleeping bag. If you're thinking of a sleeping bag for back packing, be sure to get one of the mountaineering bags. They cost more but are small and light, yet warm.

Lights. Most bike lights are adequate, but if you want more power for night off-road riding, you might try a halogen quartz headlight. These are still illegal on the road, but may win approval soon. They are much brighter than domestic models and are standard in Europe on many cars and bikes. These can be used in pairs or singly mounted on the special brackets and will cost about thirty dollars each.

Burglar alarm. Several types of burglar alarms are on the market to protect your parked cycle. A new electronic one automatically triggers a loud, pulsating alarm the instant someone tampers with your bike. It's completely self-contained, has its own batteries, and bolts on near the taillight. Some have false-alarm features. This lets the alarm shut off after a few minutes and resets itself to ring again if the vandalism or theft try is made again.

Cycle covers. A handy accessory for your bike is a cover. Many are made of heavy-gauge plastic with a cloth lining. They are durable,

Individualized accessories.

waterproof, and even fire resistant. They drop over your bike to protect it both inside and out. Most of these fold compactly and come with handy carrying cases for travel. They are made in sizes of up to 350cc models. Most firms have them to fit bikes with and without windshields.

Bumper mount carrier. A lot of riders like to drive their bikes out in the open country with the rest of the family. The best way to do this is with a bumper mounted bike carrier. Least expensive and simplest are the sturdy carriers that clamp securely onto a car's rear bumper. One wheel goes in each loop and the bike is tied against the tailgate. Look for the type that is tied down on the bottom to prevent the bounce-up problem.

So much for the bike itself—what about the rider? What clothing or equipment should you have to ride safely on your new bike?

Helmet. Leading the list must be the safety-approved helmet with chin strap and face plate. In some states you must wear a helmet to ride a motorcycle on the streets or highways. In every state it should be law, and motorcycle-riding experts say that only a fool will ride a motorcycle without an adequate crash helmet. Be sure the helmet you select is up to the Snell 70 Safety standards. Most will say on their advertising if they have been approved by official sports car and motorcycle groups. It should have a full fiberglass shell with a foam liner and nylon-covered foam-rubber upholstering. Be sure it has a chin strap. Helmets come in many styles.

Helmet shields. While the helmet is vitally important, the shield or face protection in front of the helmet is also an element you need to consider when outfitting yourself for riding.

No matter what type of helmet you buy, it will probably be equipped to take snap-on face shields. Most of these are made of tough plastic, with snaps, and can be attached to the helmet. When the shield becomes scratched or worn, it can be discarded and a new one put on. Most firms have shields for the bucket-style or full-coverage helmets. This helmet shield protects the rider completely from the neck up.

Another style of shield is the tear-away. These come in sets of five acetate sheets and are mounted directly over the regular helmet shield. In dirt track competition when the first shield gets dirty, mud-spattered,

A helmet with dirt shields.

or so that you can't see through it, you can tear the outermost one away and have a clean face shield. When it gets dirty again, you rip off the second one, and so on through the race.

One type of face shield that actually can help cut drag and wind turbulence for the rider is the bubble shield that snaps on to most helmets. This one is made by Paulson Manufacturing Corporation in Fallbrook, California. It can be used with or without the sun visor, or the shield can be purchased with a type of paint-on visor.

You've seen the football players with the chin cups on their helmet

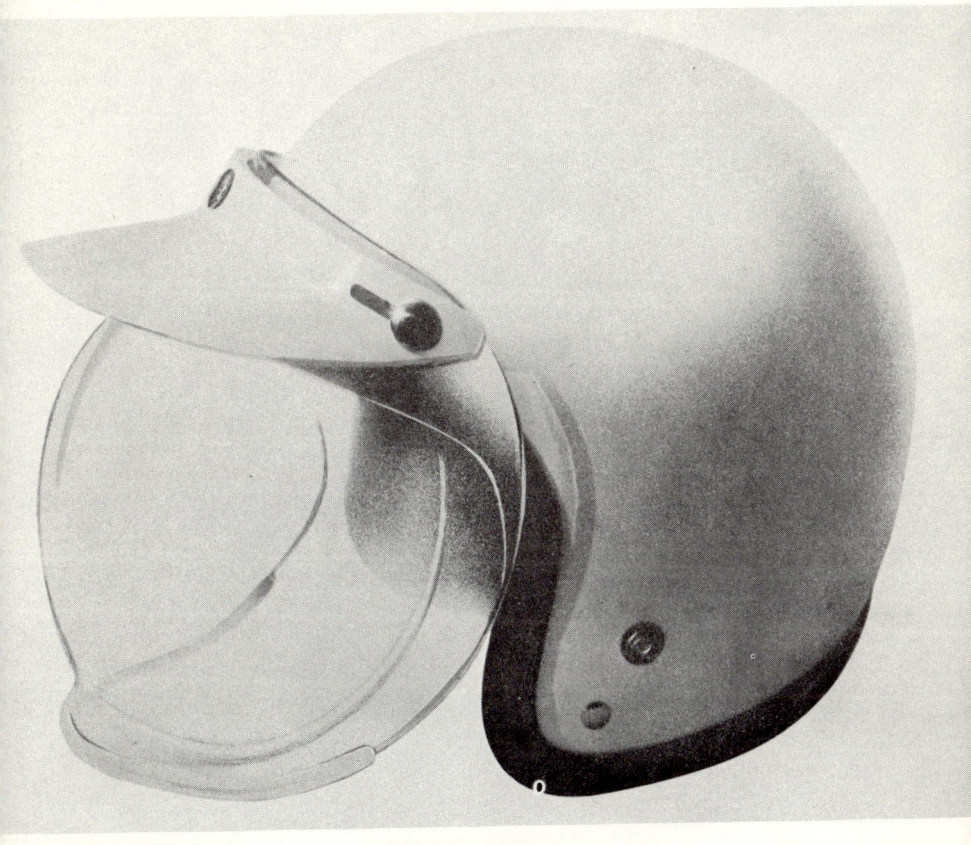

A bubble helmet.

chin straps? You can get one almost like that for your motorcycle helmet. The chin cup is made for an extra measure of comfort and protection and often can be bought in several different colors to match your helmet or bike.

If your helmet isn't fitted to take snap-on shields, or if you simply prefer another system, you can go to goggles. Many firms make these in strong polyethylene that gives you plenty of front and side vision, with a snap band around your head. They give you eye protection at a smaller cost.

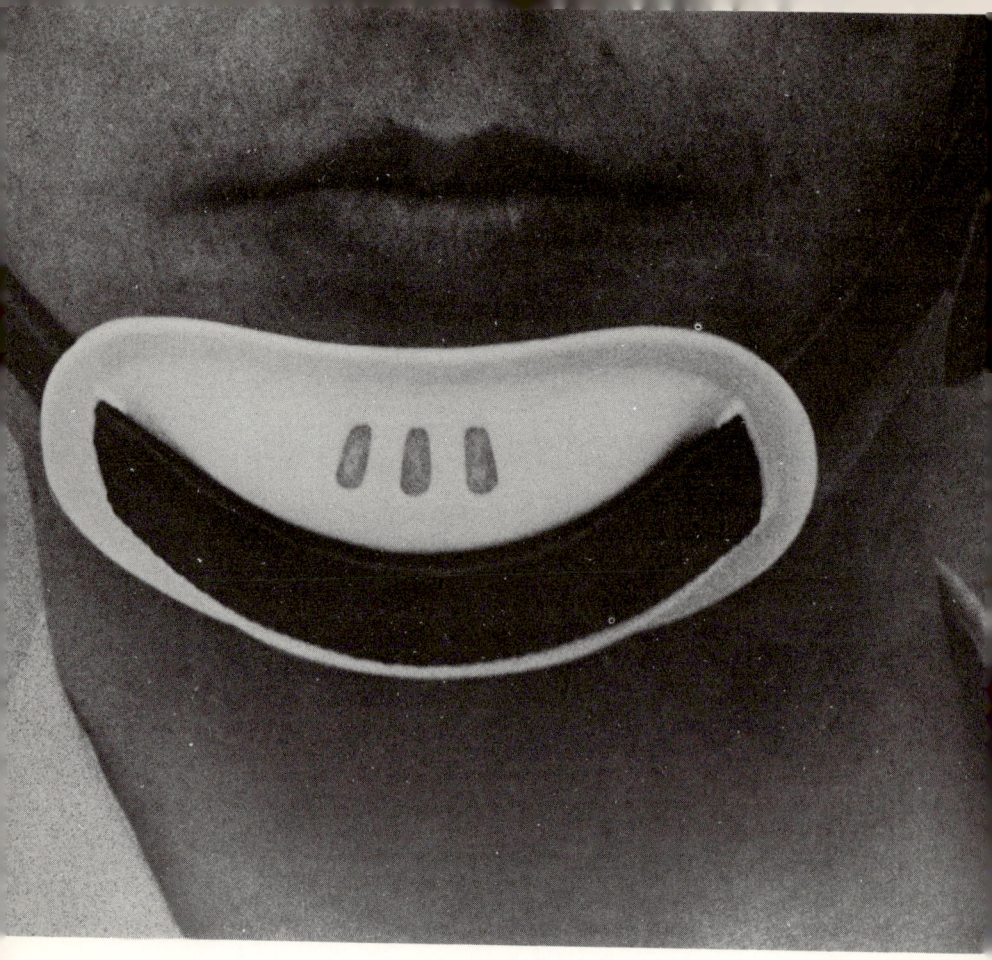

Chin strap for helmet.

What about the rest of you? Consider next a set of good riding gloves. These might be the thin leather type for hand protection or big heavy types to protect and also keep you warm on a cold, wild winter day.

Protect your feet as well. Only an idiot rides a motorcycle barefoot. Use your heaviest shoes or, better, your hiking boots. Special cycle boots are available from the road type that go seventeen inches with full zippers up the side to heavy buckled and specially made motocross boots that will run you at least fifty dollars. If you do much rid-

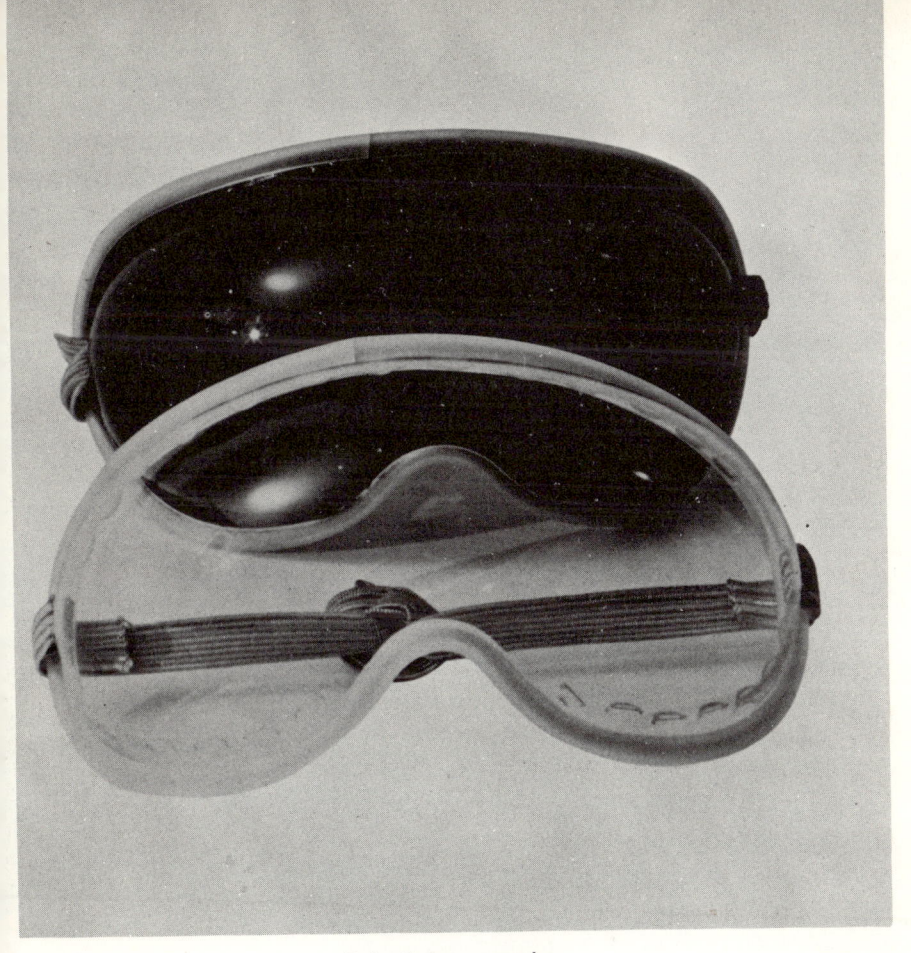

Polyethylene goggles.

ing, get some boots; they will pay for themselves in savings on bandages and broken-bone fees at the doctor's office.

If you want to go the whole way into cycling, you can get yourself a padded riding vest or move into the full jacket and pants for off-road riding protection. The ultimate in stylish road wear for cyclists are coat and pants made of leather. Called "leathers," they are very expensive, very hot in summer, and not so warm in winter. But leathers do protect your body in any spill or crash.

Section 5

Know Your Machine

Fixing your bike, taking care of it, even repairing it can be interesting and fun, but the real purpose of it all is to move out on the dirt or the pavement and ride!

When and where to ride your motorcycle brings up many problems for those who aren't legally of age. Many riders take to the boondocks and off-road trails when they are eight or ten until they are old enough.

No licenses are required in any state to ride a motorcycle off the public highway, streets, or county roads. In all fifty states riders must have a regular, valid vehicle driving license to ride these thoroughfares, but the age varies from fourteen in some states to seventeen in others.

In thirteen states you must have a regular driver's license before you can take a special motorcycle test and have your license stamped permitting you to ride on the public streets.

When these laws are strictly enforced, it turns back lots, vacant stretches of land, and many hills into off-road riding areas for the bikers too young for a street license.

Let's say you're beyond the first ride down a dirt path and that you have your car driver's license and want to get your bike street ticket. It should be easy to ride on the street after dodging boulders and ruts and brush on those off-road lots.

Once on the street, though, you face new problems, dangers, rules, and regulations. There will be many more vehicles, cars, and trucks to watch out for, different riding surfaces, and a whole saddlebag full of new skills to learn and some old ones to forget.

In the next few pages we're going to investigate some of the problems and dangers of riding on the street, to provide a street-riding handbook for the beginning motorcycle enthusiast.

Even if you've had a dozen rough country races and six years of riding off-road since you were ten, you're still a beginner in traffic and we're going to take the steps one at a time.

One caution! If you are old enough to have a license, remember that you will be driving a vehicle in a world of rules and standards where horseplay is both unwise and deathly dangerous. When you take a motorcycle on the street, you immediately assume the responsibility of obeying traffic laws, reacting in a mature manner in cases of emergency, and using your ability to drive safely and reliably at all times.

Some experts say that riding a motorcycle is more like flying an airplane than it is driving a car. And it takes at least twenty hours of instruction before you can gain your pilot's license. But most guys think they can jump on a bike, figure out where the throttle, brake, and gears are, and zoom off. Not so—not if you want to get back to your landing field in one solid chunk of bone and muscle.

In some places motorcycle schools, cycle dealerships, or city recreation or police departments give instruction in on-street motorcycle riding. If there is such an operation in your community, by all means try to get your parents to let you sign up. It will be the best training you can have. If there is no such school, ask the best rider you know to help coach you. Then with the help of the rest of this chapter, you'll be able to find out a few facts you'll need to become a responsible and safe bike rider.

The very first thing you should do when you learn to ride a bike of any kind is to know it inside out.

Read your owner's manual from cover to cover. Study it, learn where each of the pedals and switches are; learn how the bike is shifted from gear to gear, where the brakes are, how they work. Be sure you understand everything about your bike.

After you have the manual down cold, sit on the machine. Most bikes have side or center kickstands. Use a two-by-four and prop up the bike with the side kickstand on the wood. This will let you sit nearly straight up on the machine. Now dream yourself on a ride.

Do everything you would do on a ride except actually starting the motor: Shift the gears, rev the engine, make the turns, apply the brakes. Play with it; get to know the feel of the machine when it is standing still. Those same controls will feel much that way when you're zooming down a street.

If you're too young to get it on the street, this is another way you can get a head start. Dry-run it with the motor off, shifting gears, revving engine, using the brakes until you have the levers and switches and handles down pat.

This engine-off use of controls may prevent you from getting into a minor skirmish with a fence or garbage can in the alley when you forget where the brake was.

We can't tell you where your pedals and levers are, because their positions are not standardized. This will come in time, but bike manufacturers are still too individualistic and too widespread to have uniformity. But with your owner's manual, you'll have that all worked out.

You bought a secondhand bike and the previous owner lost his manual? Run down to the dealer selling that make and buy a new one. It will cost only a couple of dollars.

On gear shifting, the foot-pedal shifting bikes now have a standard

Downshifting with toes.

Folding out the kick lever.

pattern with a two-stage operation. With your toe lift the lever to change up through the gears. Then let off the pressure before trying to shift into the next higher gear. If you're going to shift down, press down with your toe and then let up on the pressure before shifting down to the next gear.

Be sure to keep your toe a half-inch in back of the shift lever between shifts. This requires you to think when you want to shift and prevents the bad habit of riding with your toe on the lever all the time, which can cause your bike to shift when you don't want it to.

Check the handlebars on your bike. Do they "fit" you? Are they in the right position, or do you have to lean too far forward? There is an adjustment you can make such as you used to do on your bicycle. Loosen the clamp bolts and rock the bar ends until they're right for you. Try to keep the handle grips parallel with the ground, since this will give you the best control of your bike. Tighten the bolts alternately a turn each until they both are locked securely in place. The control levers can also be adjusted so you can reach them easily. Loosen them at the bars and rotate them around the bars until they are comfortable, then tighten.

Now that you know your machine standing still, now that you've taken her on a hundred dry runs, consult your manual again and see what it says about starting her up.

The best spot for this is in your driveway, not on the street. Work out a pattern for starting your bike, and use it every time. Usually this will include turning on the fuel-control valve. Most bikes have three positions, "on," "off," and "reserve." Turn it to "on" and learn where the lever is by feel. Now shift into neutral and be sure it is neutral by rocking the bike.

Fold the starter lever out and set the handle against the heel of your boot. Now push the lever down smartly all the way to the bottom of the stroke. Some bikes need ot be primed before starting on cold days; some bikes need priming on even hot days. Learn how your bike reacts. When your machine starts, let the lever back up by lifting your foot slowly. Then fold the kick starter in place and out of the way.

A fashion note here. If you like bell-bottom pants, don't use them

Starting your bike.

Folding in the kick lever.

on your bike. Peg-legged jeans are better. The flapping bell bottoms can get caught on levers and even blow into the spokes of your wheel, causing a real hassle.

As you kick the starter, your right hand should be opening the throttle, usually about a quarter of a turn, and at the same time you should have the front brake on to prevent any accidental movement. If you did use the choke, be sure it's turned off before moving.

Try to get used to working the clutch and front brake handles with only your thumb and forefinger holding onto the handlebars. That leaves two or three fingers to work the brake or clutch, and sometimes both at the same time, with your thumb and other fingers holding the handlegrips.

Now, what about that first ride?

If possible, take your first ride somewhere that you won't have to worry about curbs, traffic, light poles, or complaining citizens. Ideal for the city-bound is a big parking lot on a holiday at a supermarket, at a shopping center, or maybe a big industrial lot. Remember most of these are private property and you should get permission before riding there. One good idea here is a big church parking lot. Be sure to talk to the church secretary or have your father call and ask if it would be all right. Explain about this being your first attempts and it would be much safer for you than on the street.

If you have access to a country lane with no traffic, this is a fine spot as well.

You'll need both feet and both hands to operate your motorcycle. Remember that. You must concentrate to do everything properly, especially at first. Later your hands and feet will work almost automatically, but for a while it's going to take conscious effort for control.

Riding a bike is not like driving a car. One basic difference: In a car when you go around a corner, you lean away from it so your body stays level with the roadway. When you ride around a corner on a motorcycle, you lean with the bike, keeping your body at the same angle as the machine, as you did on your bicycle. This is the toughest lesson to teach a new cycle rider. It's probably more difficult to teach an adult than a kid who remembers his bicycle riding.

A motorcycle is like a bicycle. You become a part of the machine, you are glued to it, move when it moves, sway and lean when it leans, and you function as a section of that larger unit. Then you're really riding the machine.

On your first runs, ride straight ahead. We'll say you got your machine started on the first kick, moved your shift into first gear, and kept the throttle at a quarter open as you let out on the clutch slowly.

Both your feet are on the ground, keeping you upright. Now release the hand brake. The gears mesh and move the chain. The rear wheel bites in and pushes you forward. A second later your feet come off the pavement and you're moving; you're riding your new motorcycle!

After half a dozen straight-ahead patterns, try a turn. Remember, if you have any speed at all, anything over five or six miles an hour, you do not have to "steer" your bike around a corner. All you need to do is lean, and your leaning bike will automatically go around the corner. The sharper you lean, the sharper the corner. And again, remember to lean in with the bike.

Try to keep your backbone directly over the center of your bike. Drive an imaginary pole inside your shirt and down through the center of your bike seat and along the front of the tire. When you lean one way, that pole leans with you. It won't take long to catch on to this "leaning turn." It's the basis of all motorcycle turns except a skid turn, which racers use.

Remember to push that kick starter lever back into place before you move. If you don't, you'll be licking a wounded shinbone. That's another good reason for wearing boots when you ride; they protect your ankles and shins as well as your feet.

When you put your feet down as you stop, be sure your toes point straight forward. An outward-slanting foot slides away from the bike before stopping completely.

Proper cornering.

Dragging your heels on the first ride.

For your first few runs use your whole hand on the clutch and brake levers. Use the hand brake on the front for your stop now, leaving foot braking for later.

If that first takeoff bothers you, try leaving your feet on the ground and lift your toes so just your heels skid along the pavement as you let out on the hand brake.

After a few feet you'll get the feel of it and lift your feet to the foot pegs and you're off and riding!

It might be a good idea to try just the feet-down runs. Keep the throttle at a quarter open, shift into first gear, then gently open the clutch and let off on the brake. Roll for a few feet, then pull back on the clutch and the hand brake and put your feet down for a stop. Do this several times.

If you come to the end of your parking lot, get off your bike and walk it around and head it back the other way. After several more of these try the same thing with your feet on the pegs. Then after a dozen or so trips, try a slow turn, remembering to lean.

How about shifting? That's tougher. Remember to do what you did before. You're rolling as before, feet on the pegs, but instead of the brake, pull in only the clutch, snap off the throttle, lift up on the foot lever until you hear a click into gear. Then let out slowly on the clutch. Throttle gently back on to a quarter and you'll be moving along at a faster pace.

To slow down pull back on the clutch handle, then apply your hand brake gradually, let down your feet for a gentle landing, and you're back home. Repeat this operation a dozen or so times until you can shift from first to second smoothly and naturally.

Next, as you come in for your landing, after letting off on the clutch, try touching the rear brake with your foot, and let off on the throttle. When you begin to slow, let the clutch out and ease off on the brake. Try it again until you can come almost to a wobble stop before you let off the brake and let out the clutch to pick up speed again.

All the time, remember you need to watch out where you are going and how fast you are going. Be ready to stop at any time to avoid pedestrians, other motorcycles, or cars that may wander into "your" practice parking lot.

Make it a habit to let off your rear brake just before you stop, and make the final stop with your front hand brake. This allows you a two-foot landing, for safe control of your bike. Remember that bike weighs more than you do. The Harley TX-125 weighs 228 pounds with half a tank of gas. The bigger bikes weigh from 400 pounds on up!

If you're on your own in this training course, build some "trails" and riding courses with the use of paper plates. You can nail these into the blacktop or wet them down and keep them in place. Then practice riding your course without running over any of the plates.

You might want to wet down one corner of the lot with a pail or two of water and practice riding through it. The actual puddle won't be as slippery as the tracks coming out of it. These tracks could result in a spill, particularly if the rider touched his front brake when turning through them. Learn how to ride in the wet and when to brake.

Well, there you are, your first few lessons. There are a lot of things to learn yet. So just hang on.

Pretrip inspections

A good cross-country truck driver does a pretrip inspection on his rig every morning before moving out. That's a great idea for you as well. Why? Little things loosen up, wear, and get out of position—but they happen so slowly that you don't notice them. By examining the main mechanical elements on your machine deliberately, you can tell if a nut is loose or if a spoke is broken.

It might be a good idea to work out a checklist and leave squares in back of each item so you can put a mark there when the work is done. Here are some items for your checklist:

1. Throttle twist grip. Is the rubber throttle grip on solidly and not

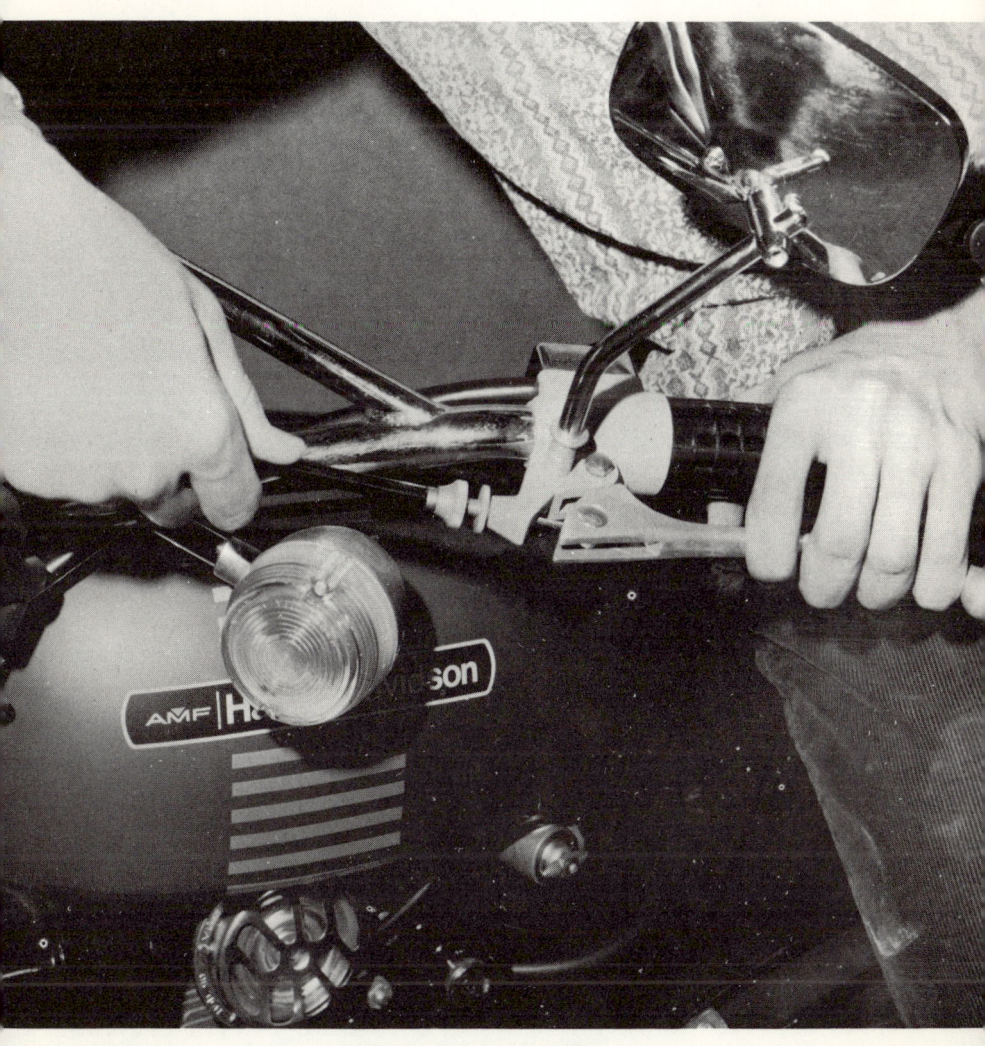

Examining the clutch cable.

split or damaged? Check the throttle cable to be sure there are no kinks or signs of wear.

2. Check the clutch cable from grip to clutch and look at both working ends to be sure there is no damage.

3. Look over the front brake handle and cables, watching for breaks or frays. Tighten the locknuts on all cable pulls.

4. Look over the rear brake pedal for cracks, as well as the foot pegs and their rubbers.

5. Check your lighting. Be sure the headlight works on both high and low beam. Shine it against a wall or watch it flick up and down as you switch it. Be sure your front and rear brake actuated lights work. Look over the turn signals to be sure they flash both front and rear and that side lights are operational.

6. Check spark plug and cable. Look to see that the cable is clean with no cracks, kinks, or frays. Be sure the plug is screwed tightly into the head.

7. Be sure to see if fuel lines are tight on the petcocks and at the carburetor.

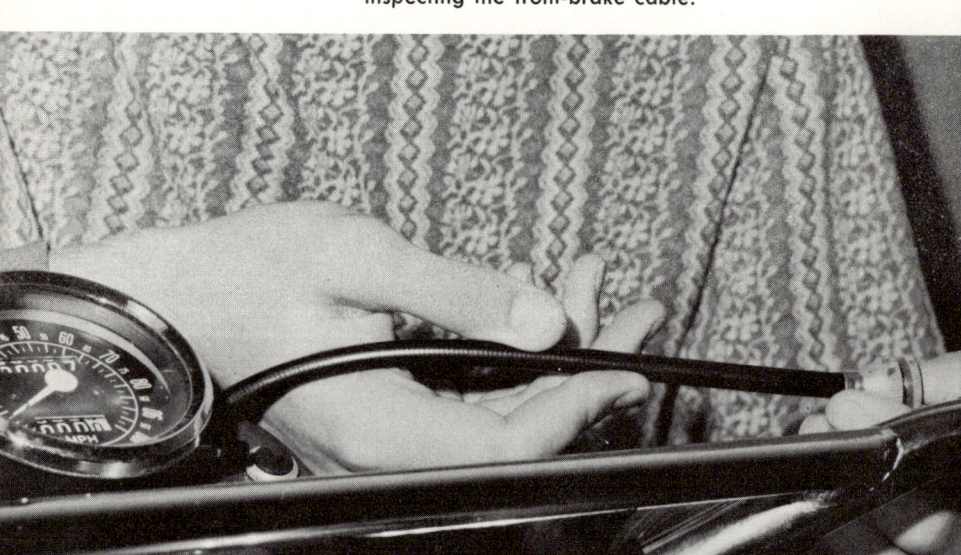

Inspecting the front-brake cable.

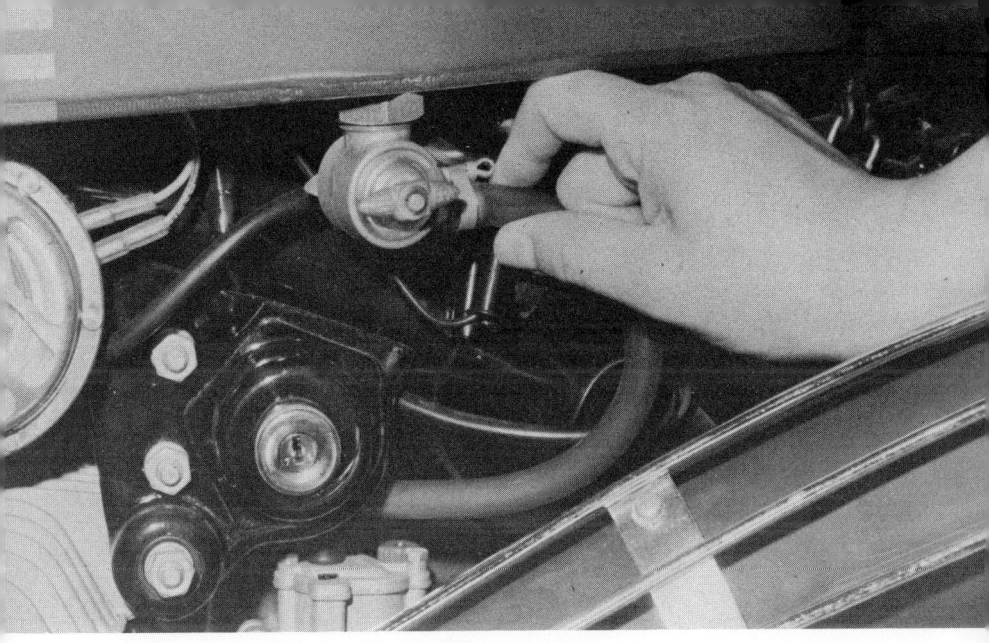

Ensuring that fuel lines are tight.

8. Front tire. Is the tire pressure correct with owner's manual recommendation? Look at the valve stem. Is it bent backward or forward? If so, let air out of the tire and fix it so valve is straight up. A leaning stem can break off. Look at the tire tread. Are there any nails or metal bits embedded or any tread chunks missing? Is the tread worn down dangerously thin? Use screwdriver and ping the spokes. If they all sound tightly metallic, fine. If one clunks, see if it's broken or only needs tightening. Don't distort rim roundness by overtightening spokes. Is the front axle nut in place and locked on?

9. Spin your front wheel to be sure the bearings are working correctly. If wheel drags, find out why.

10. Check your chain. Is it too tight, too loose? It should have only half an inch of play. Check rear axle nuts to be sure they are tight. Lift rear of bike and spin the wheel to check for wobble. Slow tire and look at tread for wear, nails, metal chips, chunking of tread as with front tire. Tap spokes with screwdriver and listen for tightness sound. Adjust any loose ones.

11. If you have a tool box under the saddle or elsewhere, check it to be sure you have your usual emergency tools. Include pliers, chain links, master chain link. Two spare spark plugs carefully wrapped to protect them. Wrench for removing front and rear wheels, plug wrench, chain-adjustment tool. Be sure to have an impact screwdriver and small hammer to loosen Phillips-headed screws that usually hold on the ignition-magneto cover.

Usually you won't be able to get these screws out with a regular screwdriver because the factory and your dealer will hammer-drive these screws in tight.

If you're taking a long ride, you might want light bulbs and fuses wrapped protectively, a spoke wrench, and a clean rag. Now you should be set.

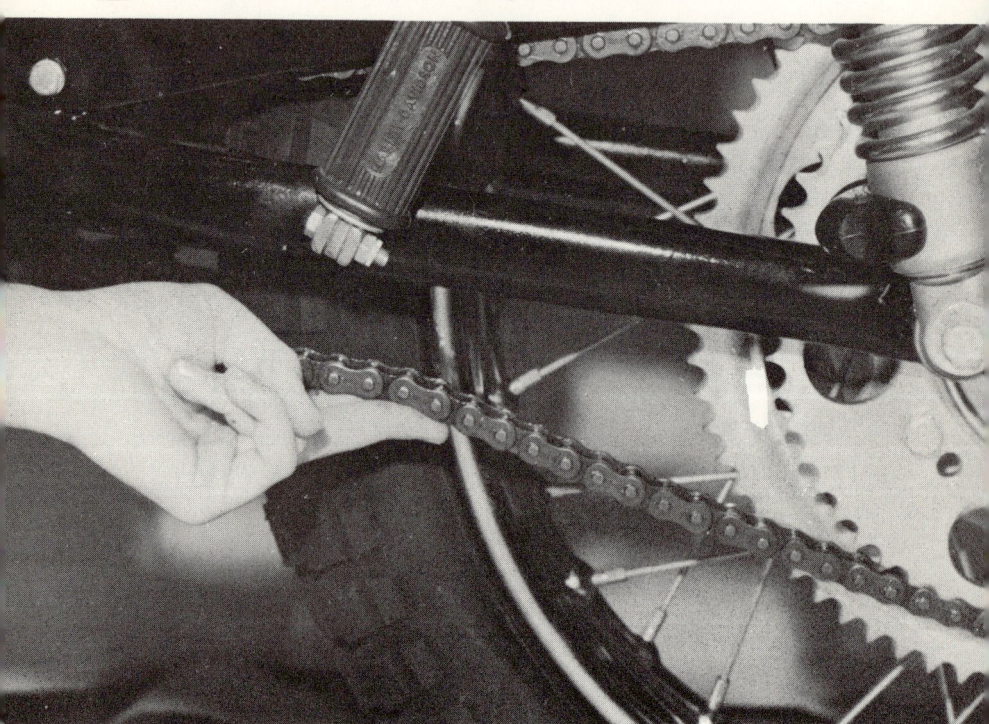

Checking chain tension.

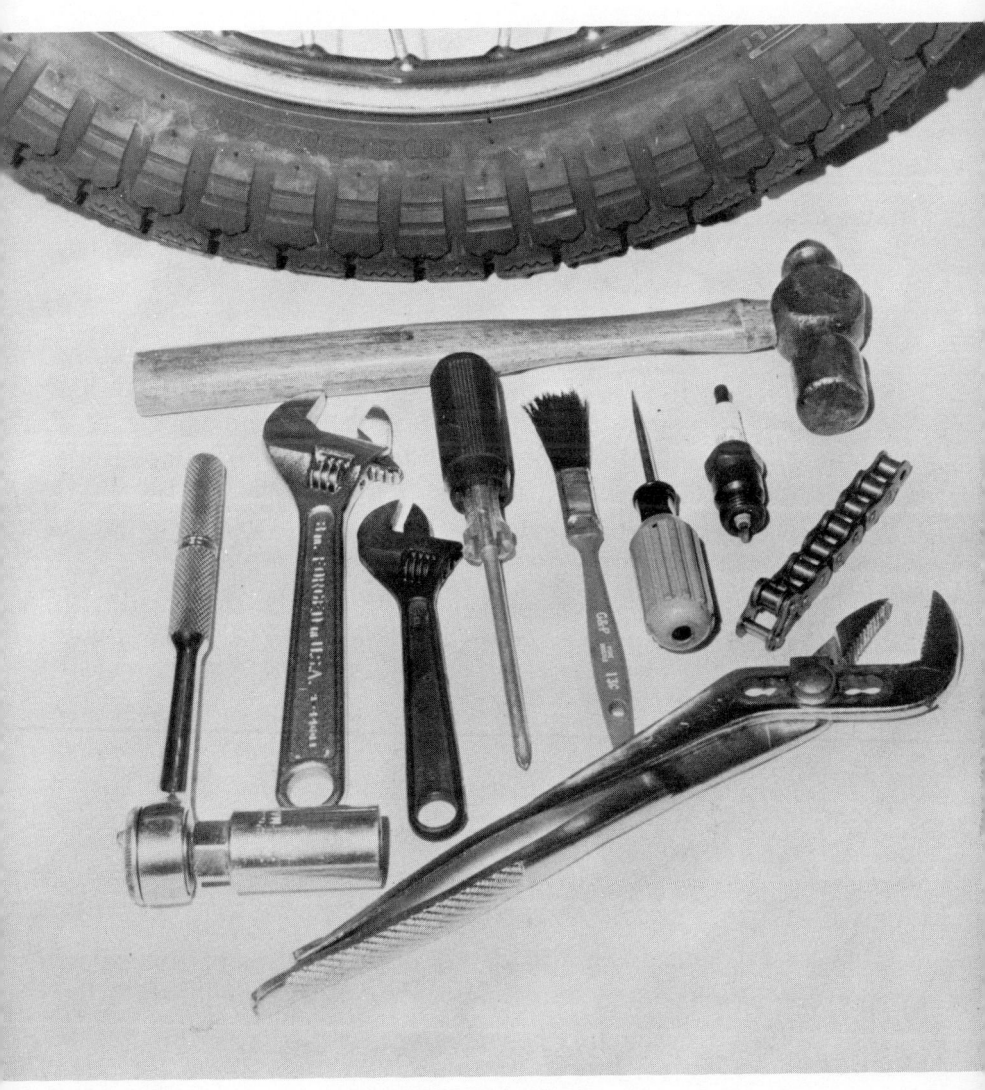

Some recommended tools.

Little lessons in bike control

Getting the hang of your bike now? Getting more confidence? Fine, but remember, this is a street bike, not built for wild cross-country rides. Still, you should take a turn at some dirt riding. It's one good way to find out what a skid feels like. Your machine is much more likely to skid in loose dirt than on pavement.

So get out in the tules and try a few slow-speed runs around the grass and the dirt roads. A flat, smooth area is best for dirt training. If the dirt is skittery, loose dirt or gravel over a hard base, it will be very slippery. Any excess throttle or brake will acquaint you with a skid. A five-miles-an-hour stop on this surface will react the way a 50-mph panic stop on pavement does.

If your rear wheel starts to skid here, keep your low-side leg off the peg and out on the dirt. Don't let the bike fall on your leg. If the bike does go down, you can hop away or drop down on that downside leg.

This is low-risk skid riding. You really shouldn't get hurt in a five- or ten-mph skid, but be careful. Learn to let the rear wheel skid a little, then steer toward the direction of the skid to help overcome it. If you don't the wheel could be jerked right out of your hands and you may be dumped over the handlebars.

The whole idea of dirt skid practice is to learn how to handle your bike in a higher-speed skid. A little bit of trying will give you the confidence you need to know what you can do with your machine and what you can't.

What about your road hazards? If you can't avoid hitting something, such as a length of two-by-four that's dropped off a truck, try to go over it in the center and at right angles to its length—straight ahead. Don't try to angle over it. The best way is to stand up on the pegs, shifting your weight more to the rear of the machine. Your knees will be slightly bent and arms straight. As soon as your front wheel goes over the obstacle, move slightly forward and sit down to maintain control.

This is the only time you should be standing on the pegs for street riding. Your motorcycle is easiest to control with your weight as low as practical on the machine, and this means sitting down.

Riding the streets

The ultimate practical use of a motorcycle is getting on the street and going somewhere—transportation. This means you're going to be moving into a world where not everyone acts predictably. This is especially true with motorists around bikes.

Many accident reports involving a car and a cyclist show that the motorist swears he or she never saw the motorcycle. This is the cardinal rule for all bike riders—ride defensively because the others on the road simply don't see you.

The best cycle rider is always alert, remembering that car drivers overlook him, and driving defensively at all times. This means giving the right of way, never demanding it, slowing down to let cars jet in front of you from stop signs, riding at the edge of the lane so you can make a quick detour out of the way of a big Buick boiling up behind you—doing everything in the book to keep out of the way of the bigger and heavier machines.

Also remember that any car on the road has the mechanical advantages over any motorcycle. The car can stop faster and take a corner faster than you can—and do it more safely. The car can stop without putting down even one foot, and an extra passenger does not throw off the control of his machine. So remember, cars have advantages over any motorcycles in these circumstances.

Does that mean you should ride scared on the streets? It wouldn't hurt a thing for the first six months.

After that you'll gain confidence, but more importantly, you'll learn

A high-powered machine.

quickly the pitfalls, traps, problems, and dangers of a busy city street. By then you'll be ready for them; you'll be reacting to a danger, perhaps before you consciously recognize it. You'll know that every motorist, pedestrian, dog, water puddle, and slick railroad track is out to get you, to put you down, to skid you along on your legs or shoulder.

Since you know this secret, you'll be ready and know how to avoid the problems.

Now, let's move on to some specific street dangers.

a. Watch out for pedestrians, especially those walking along the side of a road or those about to cross a street. You have no way of knowing what they are going to do or when they might decide to run across the street directly in front of you. Here you can group several typical hazards in the same box. Treat them the same way you would a pedestrian: range cattle grazing along the shoulder of a roadway—they could bolt into you as you come to them.

Bicycle riders are in the same group; at slow speed they often make ninety-degree turns in the street simply to keep their balance. Highly unpredictable. The last group in this hazard class is little old ladies driving Cadillacs, Lincolns, and Chryslers. If you see one coming, get as far off the street as possible.

b. Parked vehicles. Always give them a wide berth; stay at the outside of the traffic lane beside them, or to be safe, move to the far left lane as you pass the parked rigs. Again, one may pull suddenly into the street. The driver looked in his rearview mirror, saw no other car, and pulled out. Chances were in his flash look at the glass he mistook you for a pedestrian or a bicyclist half a block away.

c. A half-out vehicle. Say a car is backed or driving out of a driveway or alley. He comes part way, stops, and looks both directions to clear traffic. But don't count on his seeing you coming. Even when you have your headlight on, he probably won't see you. Watch him. If he does continue to come out, be ready to slow or turn around him. At this point know what traffic is behind you in both lanes. As soon as you see him, it's a good idea to slow down, so you can stop or simply let him wedge into traffic ahead of you. Don't ever demand your right of way. You might get it and wind up dead.

d. Keep your eyes moving. Just like a rover back in pro football, your eyes should be everywhere at once. More than one rider has prevented crashing because he just happened to see a car running a red light as he looked under a truck. Your eyes should be moving all the time like a hunter, hunting for trouble, giving you time to take accident-avoiding action.

e. Never ride in the center of a traffic lane, especially on a well-traveled road. The center is where cars drip oil and where much exhaust hits as well. Look at it; the pavement or cement will show a much darker color there, and that means oil, which can be slick and slippery even when dry. Give it a few drops of rain and you'll be going down so fast you won't even know why. Drive in the tire grooves on either side of the traffic lane.

f. Most motorcycle accidents happen as a driver coming toward you makes a left-hand turn through your lane of traffic. The driver never sees you. He doesn't know you're there, you see him coming, know he's blinking for a left, and you're sure he'll stop and wait for you. Don't bet your life on it. Always ride with your headlight on; this improves your visibility to drivers. But when you see a car about to turn left, slow down and let him go; assume that he hasn't seen you. Of course, hope that the driver behind you is watching both you and the left turner. If you wait for the illegal left turner and the car behind doesn't see you waiting, your only hope may be some kind of evasive-action left turn yourself.

g. Dogs. As with bicycles, dogs can be a real menace. Don't try to kick the mutt; don't look down at him. That will only distract your riding and might send you crashing into a parked car. Instead see the dog early (you've been looking around everywhere, remember) and estimate his planned point of attack. If he's cutting you off at the pass, just pour on the power and outdistance him, leaving him panting in your dust.

Keep alert for rocks.

Using hand signals.

h. One of your best street-safety tricks is your helmet. Anyone who rides a motorcycle without a helmet has no regard for his own safety; he's a dumb-dumb. When you buy a helmet, buy the best; be sure it meets the Safety Helmet Council of America Z-90 standard, as well as the Snell Foundation standard. Don't buy a helmet over two years old, and always replace yours every two years. Helmets start to deteriorate and weaken after that time.

i. You've heard about a jackrabbit flipping a race car out of control and off the road when the car hit the bunny? The same thing can happen to a bike. A rock the size of your fist can cause it if you don't see it. Keep alert; watch for all road hazards.

j. If you're riding over ten mph, a pair of goggles or face shield on your helmet is essential. A bug hitting your exposed eye at 40 mph can blind you for life. Always wear eye protection whenever you ride.

k. Use hand signals. When you turn or change lanes, blink your turn signals on the bike, turn your head, look behind, and then give a hand signal. Everything you do to make sure the car behind you understands what you are going to do will make it safer for you. Hand signals especially attract attention, because most car drivers never use them.

1. Watch that tailgater. Your tailgate is mighty small and not crushproof. Use your rearview mirrors and try to keep two car lengths for each ten miles an hour between the cars in front and behind you. If the driver behind insists on closing it up too much, change lanes and let him move ahead.

m. Many chunks of freeways and expressways now have "rain grooves" designed to help car tires squeeze out the water and keep better traction in wet weather. These grooves cause rumbles in your bike. Your smaller tire doesn't like them and the front rubber will set up a slight wobble. On most bikes you can sit back and let the machine correct itself: It's best not to take any corrective action, since this can result in overcontrolling and then you'll be in trouble.

n. Designed as safety markings, arrows, stripes, and signs painted

Watch the street for dark blotches.

on the street constitute one of the most treacherous parts of motorcycle riding. They are smooth and slick, and usually are in high oil-loss areas. Stay to one side of the painted markers on any traffic lane.

o. If you have problems with your bike and must get off the road or street, be sure you get your machine well out of any possible traffic area. In town put it on the sidewalk if possible. On a country road get well off the shoulder if practical. Don't get yourself clobbered by a car slamming around a corner and another driver who "just didn't see you."

p. Avoid metal surfaces on a street. Most of these will be manhole covers, which can be slick as ice if they have a little bit of rain or early-morning dew on them. Ride around these, not over them.

q. Railroad tracks should be crossed cautiously and at right angles to the tracks. If the rails slant across the road, use all of your lane to angle into them so you can take them properly.

r. Visually check every street. If it has dark black blotches on it, be alert. It may be fresh tar or potholes recently filled with fresh macadam. Either one will mean trouble for you if you try to zoom over them too fast or make the slightest turn or braking action on them. Slow down and take the area at a safe speed.

Watch for black strips of tar on macadam roads. It might be a "sealing" job that was put down years ago—but it also might be a gooey, fresh tar stripe that can wipe you out faster than it takes to tell it. Ride around any area of the road that looks different.

s. New tar? Watch out where a road crew is putting down new liquid tar and sand/rock cover or laying a thick mat of blacktop. Usually there is a bump or ridge down the center of the road and another where you go up or down from the new surface to the old one. Be ultracautious here, since the asphalt is only semiset and that ridge and bump can cause you trouble.

Section 6

Which Motorcycle For You?

Whether you're on the street with your own bike or just wishing that you could get there, this far along in your motorcycling experiences you know quite a bit about cycles and how to ride them. Now the big question comes up, which is best for you?

More than fifty different brands are sold in the United States today. Some of them sell only a few models and a few bikes. Others such as Harley-Davidson, Suzuki, Honda, and Yamaha sell hundreds of thousands of motorcycles.

A working bike.

Among these fifty different makes there is a bike that is just right for you, right for your age and experience, right for the type of riding that you want to do, and right for the amount of cash that you have to spend.

If you haven't zeroed in on one make or model bike yet, perhaps we can help you decide by showing some representative models that will at least indicate the spread of the types of wheels available.

Probably the safest of all of the motorbikes is the ATC. This is the tricycle with big tires and known as an All Terrain Cycle or, in some makes, an ATV, for All Terrain Vehicle. Typical is the Honda ATC-90 K1. These machines are fine for a young person's first motor-driven vehicle. They are built for off-road use, but are ultimately safe and slow and can be ridden over sand and mud and grass and gravel with equal ease. Some with all three large tires are just as at home on snow as on dirt. Easy to ride, no balance problem, and comparatively slow.

A minibike.

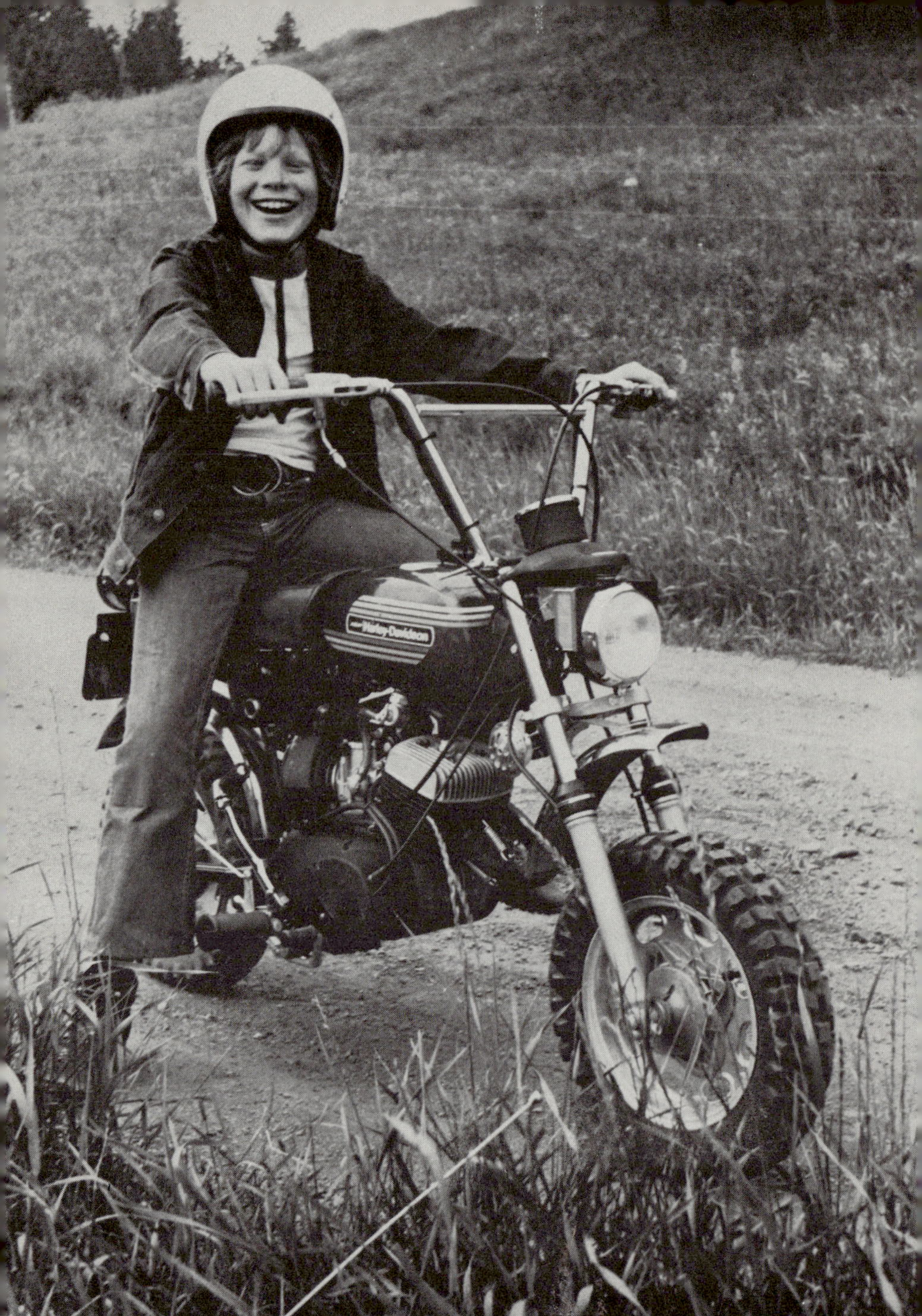
Harley-Davidson

Minibikes

Next up the ladder is the minibike. These are made by many firms and most are not legal on the streets. They have small-diameter wheels, sit close to the ground, and have 50 to 90cc engines. Many of these little rigs do not have street equipment such as lights, turn signals, sidelights, etc. Plan on using them strictly off-road, where the seven to ten-year-old can have a lot of fun with them. Again they are a good rig for your first motor-driven vehicle. Typical here might be the Kawasaki 75cc minitrail.

In the same size some of the minibikes do have streetable equipment; so decide which one you want, fit for the street and fun off-road or only for off-road.

Remember here that if you get an off-road machine, you still must register it in most states. Some states offer an off-road license and registration. For this you usually don't get license plates, but rather a little sticker to put on your fender. If you register for on-road you're legal off-road as well.

The next step up is the larger, more powerful trail and street machine in the 75–100cc class. These are made either for dirt riding or for street and offer more power and longer rides. All have the large motorcycle wheel and are a second-step bike for many young riders.

Dirt bikes

From the minibikes you jump into the dirt bikes, or the off-road critters. These include bikes in the 50 to 250cc class and are built by almost all of the big-line motorcycle makers. These bikes are strictly

Dirt competition bike.

Dirt bike.

Trail bikes.

for the boondocks with no headlights, taillights, or other streetable gear. To get these bikes out to the boonies you have to put them in a trailer, a pickup, or on a rear-bumper carrier. You can't ride these on the street to get to your off-road racing places.

The happy answer to the transport problem is the on/off road bike. These are made by most manufacturers as well and come in a wide variety of power and options from about 70cc right on up to 350cc. The on/off road bike is easy to spot. It's the street-looking machine with the high front fender, where the fender is raised about eight to ten inches off the tire to give the front tire plenty of springing room when the going gets rough. The front tire on a strictly dirt bike looks the same, but the clue here is the lights on the on/off road machine. It has full streetable equipment including lights, horn, etc., so it can function in the wilds or on Park Avenue with equal ease. The on/off road will have a license tag and registration for the state, of course, and is a good combination machine.

While it is ruggedly built to take the punishment of the trail, it is also heavy and solid to give you a good, clean ride on the flat, smooth pavement. The Harley-Davidson TX-125 is an example of the on/off road machine.

Road bikes

The last large category of types of motorcycles is the road bike, the machine built strictly for rolling down the streets and highways that wants to keep out of the dirt and grime of the dirt track.

These bikes make up the majority of motorcycles in this country. They are the ones you see on the streets and might range from an Indian to a BMW, a BSA to a Kawasaki or a Suzuki or Triumph, a Honda to a Harley. Power options here are from a low of somewhere in the 100 to 125cc, to 900cc engines producing 77 horsepower. In a class by itself is the Harley-Davidson FLH-1200 with 1200cc's of power and

A bike travels easily.

Road bike.

room enough for lots of luggage racks and fairings. This is the bike many motorcycle policemen use for power and safety. It packs in 103 horsepower.

The road bike is built for comfort, safety, and convenience, which means good power and smooth cornering. They come in one-, two-, three- and four-cylinder models.

Some firms put out bikes they call "trail" models. These usually are a combination between dirt bikes and on/off road bikes, some designed strictly for nonroad use, but not dirt racing, and others that will go on or off the road.

There you have the whole story—some ways to service and repair your bike and instructions for riding one of these critters, so you can have years of happy riding.

Index

Accessories, 67-77
Accidents, avoidance of, 99-107. *See also* Safety
Air cleaner
 and engine trouble, 45
 maintenance of, 12, 14, 57, 60
All Terrain Cycle, 111
Automatic advance unit, 44-45

Backfiring, causes of, 44
Balance
 in cornering, 88
 and motorcycle type, 111
 in skidding, 88
Battery, 29
 charging, 58-59
 and ignition trouble, 41,43-44, 58
 maintenance of, 20,23,58-59,63
 storage of, 56, 58-59
Bikes. *See* Motorcycles
Brake lights, 94
Brakes
 adjustment of, 31,34
 inspection of, 94
 operation of, 87,92, 107
 trouble-fixing, 53

Carbon buildup
 and engine trouble, 45
 removal of, 20

Carburetor
 and engine trouble, 44-45
 and ignition trouble, 44
 maintenance of, 17, 57
 trouble-fixing, 14, 46, 48
Chilton Book Company, 54, 56
Chin cups and straps, 73-75
Choke
 adjustment of, 48
 operation of, 87
Choppers, 67, 71
Circuit-breaker points, 29
 adjustment of, 18, 26-27
 maintenance of, 18, 26
Clothing, 73-77
 leather, and safety, 77
 for off-road riding, 77
Clutch, 94
 operation of, 87, 91
 trouble-fixing, 43, 50-51
Clymer Publications, 56
Condenser, 29
 and electrical trouble, 54
 and engine trouble, 45
 and ignition trouble, 42
 replacement of, 27
Contact breaker points
 and ignition trouble, 42, 43
 trouble-fixing, 54
Control cable, adjustment of, 34
Control levers, adjustment of, 84

Controls, operation of, 81-87
Cornering, 60, 87-88; and tire wear, 59
Crankshaft, 41
Customization, 67-73
Cycle covers, 71,73
Cylinder, painting, 57-58
Cylinder exhaust port, maintenance of, 20
Cylinder head bracket, and engine vibration, 53

Degreasers, 58
Dirt bikes. *See* Off-road bikes
Dirt skid practice, 98
Drive chain
 and brake adjustment, 31
 and engine vibration, 53
 inspection of, 95
 maintenance of, 23-24
 and noise, 53
 replacement of, 23-24, 31
Driveline, trouble-fixing, 48-51

Electrical system, trouble-fixing, 54-56
Engine
 maintenance of, 16-18, 57
 painting, 57-58
 trouble-fixing, 41-46
  compression, 20, 41, 45
  detonation, 45
  flooding, 42
  ignition, 41-44
  knocking, 20, 39, 41
  misfiring, 44
  overheating, 45
 tune-up, 26-27
 types of, 113, 116
Engine vibration, 53
Equipment, street, 116
Exhaust pipe, 20
Exhaust ports, 45-46
Expressways, riding on, 60, 65, 105

Face shield, 105
Fairings, 69
Fenders, 116
Flares, 63
Flooding
 carburetor, 46
 engine, 42

Foot pedals
 and brake adjustment, 34
 and gear shifting, 84
Footwear, 76, 88
Frame, trouble-fixing, 53
Front fork, 67
 lubrication of, 31, 53
 trouble-fixing, 53
Fuel, 59
Fuel inlet valve, 46
Fuel line
 blockage of, 14, 41
 inspection of, 94
 trouble-fixing, 41-42, 46-48
Fuel mixture, 17
 and carburetor trouble, 46-48
 and engine trouble, 45, 46
 and ignition trouble, 43
Fuel strainer
 and carburetor trouble, 48
 maintenance of, 14
Fuel-supply valve, 42, 84

Gas cap, 59
Gears. *See* Shifting gears; Transmission
Generator. *See* Magneto generator
Gloves, 76
Goggles, 75, 105
Grease, removal of, 58. *See also* Lubrication

Hand signals, 105
Handbrake, 34, 91
Handlebars, adjustment of, 84-87
Hang-ons, 69-71
Harley-Davidson Singles, 56
Harley-Davidson TX-125, 12, 29, 31, 34, 37, 43, 92
Head, painting, 57-58
Headlights, 102
 halogen quartz, 71
 sealed beam, 35
Helmet shields, 73-74
 bubble, 74
 tear-away, 73
Helmets, 73; and safety, 105
Honda ATC-90 K1, 111
Horns, 63

Idling, 63; faulty, 44, 45

Ignition circuit, 57
Ignition coil, 27, 42, 45
Ignition system, 27. *See also* Timing
   testing, 29
   trouble-fixing, 41-44
Inlet lever, 48
Inspection checklist, 92-96

Jump starting, 58

Kawasaki 75cc minitrail, 113
Kick starter, 84
   and engine trouble, 44
   sticking, 51
Kickstand, 81
Knocking, causes of, 20, 39

Lubrication, 56. *See also* Oil
   drive chain, 23-24
   engine fork, 31

Magneto generator
   and battery trouble, 42
   maintenance of, 29
   trouble-fixing, 54
Maintenance, 11-24, 59-65
   air cleaner, 12-14, 57
   battery, 20-23, 58-59,63
   circuit-breaker points, 18
   drive chain, 23-24
   engine, 16- 17, 57-58
   fuel strainer, 14
   magneto generator, 29
   muffler, 20
   oil pump, 16
   spark plug, 17-18, 39
   tire, 34-35, 95
   transmission, 37
   wheel, 95
Minibikes, 113
Misfiring, causes of, 44, 45
Motorcycles
   accesories for, 67-77
   cleaning, 56-58
   clothing and equipment for, 73-77
   customization of, 67-73
   licensing and regulation of, 69, 73, 79-80, 113, 116
   maintenance of, 11-24, 59-65

painting, 57-58
repairing, 25-59
riding, 59-65, 77, 79-80, 81-92
safety and, 60, 87, 92, 99-107
service manuals for, 54-56
storing, 54, 56, 59
transporting, 73
trouble-fixing, 39-56
types of, 12, 109-119
Muffler
   and engine trouble, 45, 46
   and motorcycle regulations, 67, 69
   maintenance of, 20

Nozzle system, 46

Off-road bikes, 12, 111, 113-116
   headlights for, 71
   transporting, 73
Oil, 43-44, 56, 58. *See also Fuel mixture*
   engine, 18, 26, 44, 45, 63
   fork, 31, 53, 63
   transmission, 37, 51, 63
Oil pump, 45; maintenance of, 16-17
On/off-road bikes, 12, 116
Overheating, causes of, 45
Owner's manual, 12, 14, 20, 31, 34, 53, 81, 84, 95

Pack systems, 71
Paint, 57-58, 69; and degreasers, 58
Paulson Manufacturing Corporation, 74
Piston, 45
Points. *See* Circuit-breaker points
Practice courses, 92
Priming, 84

Racing, 73-74
Riding, 60, 65, 73, 77-80
   corners and turns, 60, 87-88
   dry runs, 80-87
   expressway, 60, 65, 105
   first runs, 87-92
   long-distance, 65, 69
   off-road, 77, 98
   practice, 98
   street, 60, 63, 65, 77, 98, 99-107
Road bikes, 116-119
Road hazards, 98-99, 102, 105, 107

Saddlebags, 69-71
Safety, 60, 77, 80, 99-107
   clothing and equipment for, 73-77
   first runs and, 87
   stopping and, 91-92
Service manuals, 25, 54-56
Shifting gears, 81-84, 91
Shock absorber, 53
Skidding, 98
Sleeping bags, 71
Spark plug, 94
   and engine trouble, 45
   and ignition trouble, 42, 43
   maintenance of, 17-18, 26, 39
   replacement of 17-18
Spark-plug cable, 94
   and engine trouble, 45
   and ignition trouble, 44
Starter lever, 51, 84, 87
Stopping, 88; and rear brake, 92
Storage procedures, 56-58, 59
Street bikes, 12, 67-69, 98, 113

Throttle
   and cornering, 60
   and starting, 84
Throttle grip, 16, 92-94
Timing
   adjustment of, 26-27
   and engine trouble, 44, 45
   and ignition trouble, 42
Tire pressure, 34-35, 95
   and ride quality, 58
   and weather, 59-60
   and wheel vibration, 53

Tires, 105
   maintenance of, 34-35, 58, 95
   and motorcycle storage, 56-57
   repair of, 34
Tools, 63, 96
Trail bikes, 12, 119. *See also* Off-road bikes
Transmission, 41
   maintenance of, 37
   trouble-fixing, 51
Trouble-fixing, 39-56
   brakes, 53
   carburetor, 46-48
   driveline, 48-51
   electrical system, 54
   engine, 41-46
   frame, 53
   fuel line, 41, 46-48
   ignition system, 41-44
Turn signals, 63, 94

Valves
   and engine trouble, 45
   and ignition trouble, 43

Weather
   and battery maintenance, 58-59
   and priming, 84
   and tire maintenance, 59
Wheel alignment, 53
Wheel bearings, 57, 95; repacking, 34
Wheel vibration, 53
Wheels, 113
   maintenance of, 34, 53, 56, 95
   removal of, 34

The Author

CHET CUNNINGHAM is a free-lance writer who has done numerous articles on motorcycles, automobiles and trucks, as well as a guide to automobile maintenance and handling, *Your Wheels,* published by Putnam's in 1973. He was born in Nebraska, grew up in Oregon, where he picked strawberries to earn money to buy his first bike, and was educated at Pacific University and Columbia University's School of Journalism. His wife and three children live with him in San Diego.

The Author

CHET CUNNINGHAM is a free-lance writer who has done numerous articles on motorcycles, automobiles and trucks, as well as a guide to automobile maintenance and handling, *Your Wheels,* published by Putnam's in 1973. He was born in Nebraska, grew up in Oregon, where he picked strawberries to earn money to buy his first bike, and was educated at Pacific University and Columbia University's School of Journalism. His wife and three children live with him in San Diego.